Metaphorical Stories for Child Therapy

Metaphorical Stories for Child Therapy

Of Magic and Miracles

Pat Pernicano, PsyD

JASON ARONSON
Lanham • Boulder • New York • Toronto • Plymouth, UK

Published by Jason Aronson
An imprint of Rowman & Littlefield Publishers, Inc.
A wholly owned subsidiary of The Rowman & Littlefield Publishing Group, Inc.
4501 Forbes Boulevard, Suite 200, Lanham, Maryland 20706
http://www.rowmanlittlefield.com

Estover Road, Plymouth PL6 7PY, United Kingdom

British Library Cataloguing in Publication Information Available

Library of Congress Cataloging-in-Publication Data

Pernicano, Pat, 1954–
Metaphorical stories for child therapy : of magic and miracles / Pat Pernicano.
p. ; cm.
Includes bibliographical references and index.
ISBN 978-0-7657-0781-9 (cloth : alk. paper)
1. Child psychotherapy. 2. Metaphor. 3. Narrative therapy. I. Title.
[DNLM: 1. Mental Disorders—psychology. 2. Mental Disorders—therapy.
3. Adolescent. 4. Child. 5. Metaphor. 6. Psychotherapy—methods.
WS 350.2 P452m 2010]
RJ505.S75P47 2010
618.92'8914—dc22

2010005741

∞™ The paper used in this publication meets the minimum requirements of American National Standard for Information Sciences—Permanence of Paper for Printed Library Materials, ANSI/NISO Z39.48-1992.

Printed in the United States of America

Contents

Acknowledgments

I want to thank Julie Kirsch (editorial director), Abigail Graber (editorial assistant), and Janice Braunstein (assistant managing editor) of Rowman & Littlefield for guiding me efficiently through the publishing process.

Also, were it not for the encouragement of my colleagues at Seven Counties Services, who *piloted* the original stories with their clients, this publication might never have come to pass. Scott Salathe (child CBT), Vivian Levin (preschool group), Kelly Goforth (developmentally delayed teens group), Jean Romano (expressive therapy), Laura Byrd (adult therapy), Shay Kirkpatrick (Ericksonian hypnosis), Anita Putnam (depressed women's group), and Sara Southard (expressive art therapy) demonstrated that the stories were useful with a wide variety of clinical populations.

I dedicate this book to my clients and my children, Becky and Sam, without whom there would be no stories. The characters in the stories have become dear to my heart—but never as dear as those who have so freely shared their lives with me! I hope you find treasures in these stories and experience the *magic* of insight within these pages. Many thanks to my husband, Kevin, for his hours of proofreading, as he has been a "treasure" in my life for as long as I have known him!

Introduction

The Magic of Metaphor

There is a certain *magic* to metaphor, a literary technique used within many psychotherapy conceptual frameworks. Narrative therapy, hypnosis (Ericksonian and traditional), mindfulness, neuro-linguistic programming (NLP), dialectical behavior therapy (DBT), cognitive behavioral therapy (CBT), play therapies, expressive therapies, and solution-oriented approaches all use metaphor in their interventions. Metaphor and storytelling have been used, for example, in seeding possibilities, making meaning, presenting alternative views, restructuring cognition, and reframing narrative history. Storytelling, like play, communicates with children on multiple levels. Stories and their characters serve as models, teach values and skills, and provide insight on both a conscious and non-conscious level.

In the late 1970s, there were few evidence-based child play therapy techniques available. I began using storytelling at that time in the form of mutual storytelling, a technique developed by child psychiatrist Richard Gardner (Gardner, 1971). The technique is simple. The therapist listens to a story that the child relates and identifies core themes/metaphors and how the child solves problems and resolves interpersonal conflict. Then, the therapist tells the same (or parallel) story, but with a slightly more adaptive, solution-oriented, mentally healthy, mature ending. The therapist helps the child understand and connect the stories to his or her life.

I often use the squiggles technique as a component of storytelling. I'm not sure where or how I first heard of squiggles. In an Internet search of *Squiggles Art*, I discovered that it has been used in the classroom for teaching flexible thinking, as an art activity, and in therapeutic settings. According to Schaefer and O'Connor (1983), the technique may have been developed first by Winnicott in 1971, but it was adapted by Claman in 1980 to incorporate Gardner's mutual storytelling technique. Game-like interventions, including squiggles, have long been used to deal with resistance to traditional talking, insight-oriented therapies.

Metaphor and storytelling are tools with which a therapist can gain access to the inner world of a child and use that understanding to help the child make sense of his or her world and change thoughts, feelings, and behaviors. I found that stories helped my young clients more quickly recognize and acknowledge their problems. By working on a story "character's" problems (and sometimes by talking to puppets about the problems), a child would begin to address his or her parallel problems.

During my internship in 1985, I was formally trained in clinical hypnosis for conditions such as pain and stress. But it was Bill O'Hanlon's 1993 workshop on the use of solution-oriented hypnosis that helped me understand that individuals in trance states can see things differently and gain valuable insight, propelling them toward change. A client in a trance state is in a receptive frame of mind, making it easier to shift/alter perception and restructure cognition. Dr. O'Hanlon's use of solution-oriented language, positive and negative trance induction, and metaphor were compelling in the videotapes he showed, especially a case where he guided an eating disordered client to confront her *eating monster* while looking in a mirror. My story *The Twin in the Mirror* was written years later using the same powerful metaphor.

After attending a number of solution-oriented hypnosis and Milton Erickson–enriched trainings with individuals such as Michael Yapko and Jeffrey Zeig, I realized few resources were available along those lines for children and adolescents. I sought something like Lemony Snicket's children's series *A Series of Unfortunate Events*—rich, memorable, even humorous characters and stories that could seed client change through suggestion, use of possibility language, and utilization.

As my interest in metaphor grew, I began writing down my own client stories and sharing them with colleagues. I was surprised at the ways in which the stories were used: to encourage reading and discussion with learning-disabled readers; as homework between therapy sessions; in school special education classrooms for self-esteem development; in group therapy as themes for a puppet show; and with developmentally delayed adults and teens. Some therapists used the stories with their adult clients, and many enjoyed reading the stories themselves *just for fun*.

There have been a number of evidence-based practices developed for children and families, including the *RAINBOW Program* for bipolar disordered children and teens (Pavuluri); Kendall and Hedtke (2006) *Coping Cat* (cognitive behavioral treatment for anxious children); *Trauma Focused CBT* (Cohen et al. 2003); *Functional Family Therapy* (Alexander); *Filial Play*

Therapy (Gurney 1964); and *Parent Child Interaction Training* (Hershel et al. 2002).

There are a number of child and adult treatment books available on the use of metaphor in therapy. The metaphor books for child treatment tend to focus on one problem, such as ADHD, Asperger's disorder, or OCD. These are useful, but a collection of stories will give practitioners more flexibility. The stories in most metaphor collections are brief and focused on the metaphor itself, with little character development, making the stories less memorable. I have been told that the stories in this book are *unique* because the special, *memorable* characters become *personal* to the client.

In my office recently, a 10-year-old boy picked up a smooth stone. "I remember this," he said. "We used it in our group." He was right, but the group in which we read the story (*The Magic Stone*) had met over a year ago. He went on to describe what he had done in that group and how he had used the stone to manage his anxiety.

Some themes in the stories in this volume are universal, in that they are applicable to a wide range of clients, each of whom will take what he or she needs from the story and use it to *springboard* into therapy work. Other story themes are tied to diagnostic issues, with focused treatment suggestions.

This collection of metaphorical stories is written at a second- to third-grade reading level, although the stories can be paraphrased for younger children. The stories plant seeds for the possibility of change, and *The Bottom Line* at the end of each story provides, in a *nutshell*, a new way of looking at an old problem. In using metaphor, regardless of theoretical orientation, the therapist generally does one or more of the following after conceptualizing the client's or family's core issues and barriers to change.

Select and use with a client a story

1. With a character that resembles the client in some way based on personality, behavior, or diagnosis.
2. Whose theme is parallel to some event in the client's own life.
3. That portrays a character with the client's struggle, ambivalence, or decision area.
4. That models someone solving a problem similar to the client's.
5. That models a character coming to some insight about his or her life (client has need for insight in that area).
6. That plants a suggestion therapist sees as potentially useful for the client (to get past resistance or help client see something in a new way).
7. That gives the client or family a message the therapist would like to give but the therapist suggests it will be rejected if offered "directly."
8. That gives a child opportunity to notice his or her parent's behavior in the story.

9. That gives a child/parent an opportunity to notice himself or herself in the story.
10. That gives a parent an opportunity to notice his or her child in the story.
11. That gently opens up as-yet unrecognized, non-conscious emotional material.

Generally I do not *say* anything about the story before I read it other than I thought of a story the client might relate to and I ask permission to read it in session. What follows in the session will be based on the response the client gives to the story.

For example, a young girl liked the therapist's stories so much that she came into session early in treatment wanting to tell one of her own. The therapist typed her story as she dictated it during the session and she selected clip art illustrations. She told about puppies that got separated from their parent dogs and her story provided insight into her strong feelings of anxiety about having been separated from her mother and placed out of the home. She ended the story abruptly at the end of the session and left it hanging, saying she would finish it at home. The girl continued to come to sessions each week saying that she just "could not" finish the story yet.

Several months later, the therapist noted that she was feeling much more secure living back with her mother and said, "You know, I have thought a lot about your story of the puppies. I don't know how you will choose to end it, but I almost imagine an ending where the puppies somehow find their way back home from the animal shelter and realize their mother has been looking for them the whole time." She nodded her head with a big smile and proceeded to finish her story in that session.

Whatever conceptual framework is adopted by the therapist, metaphorical stories open up "right brain," creative, intuitive processes in which clients may identify with one or more of the story's characters. There is often an "*aha*" of self-discovery, followed by open discussion of the client-character similarities. According to Zeig, using metaphor is like leading a client to a series of dots and then watching while the client "cleverly" connects them.

The stories in Part I contain general solution-oriented themes that are applicable to a wide variety of persons and problems. Part II stories address specific treatment or diagnostic issues. Each story includes a brief introduction about how the story may be used and with which types of clients. I have included Take-It-Home Questions that parallel the ideas and themes in each of the stories. The questions are most useful when used as therapy "homework" or to jump-start discussion during the session.

For most children 8 to 10 years old, the therapist will read the stories to the child. When reading with families, it is good to pass the book around so that each person takes a turn reading. After finishing the story, the therapist may invite the child to enter into puppet play, discussion, or art activity. With children 4 to 7, or developmentally challenged persons, the story themes may be used, but they need to be shortened and simplified.

When children say, "That sounds like me!" an appropriate reply might be, "Really? How is X like you?" or "Could you tell me about that?" Therapist can use the child as an expert and ask such questions as, "What do you think that character should do? How does he feel? What could we do to help him?"

In my work with children, I often offer puppets to act out a story; or after reading, I use puppets to help the child work on a treatment issue that is connected with the story.

Therapists can use puppets to model and coach, teach new behaviors, express feelings, confront or challenge beliefs, ask for help, or clarify the child's feelings and perceptions. Puppets may be used in roles such as protagonist, antagonist, or helper. The therapist may ask the puppet questions (or a puppet may ask the child questions) in order to personalize the details of the stories. The child can "help" the puppet with his/her problems, or the puppet can "help" the child. Children often whisper "truths" to puppets that they have not yet voiced.

Older children (ages 11 to 12) and teens may read the stories themselves in family, group, or individual sessions. They clearly *get* the parallel with their own lives. Some teens resist formal therapy, and stories allow them to reduce defensiveness in order to express feelings and explore their life experiences and personal coping.

Even adult clients will relate to the stories and metaphors in this book. Adults who continue to deal with childhood issues such as neglect, abuse, or abandonment may find that the stories help them think about the past in new ways.

Therapists of all theoretical orientations are encouraged to use these stories, especially early in the treatment process. The memorable and sometimes poignant characters will provide clients insight into their problems through the "aha" of personal identification; and *plant seeds* that springboard clients less defensively into the change process.

I

GENERAL TREATMENT ISSUES

1

Attention Seeking

The Proud Peacock

Henry, the main character in *The Proud Peacock,* will remind many readers of someone they have known, child or adult, and his antics will bring a chuckle; but it can be an annoying situation to be confronted by someone who is unable to recognize the impact of his or her intrusive behavior on others.

This story was written for use in a group in which one particular member interrupted others and brought every conversation back to her own issues. Group members were visibly frustrated, but none dared to confront her.

The story allowed group members to discuss ways each of them had difficulty being a good listener or paying positive attention to others. The targeted client was able to talk about her neediness and how she unintentionally pushed others away. The other group members were then able to give her feedback about her behavior and provide suggestions for change.

In one child's group, the children discussed how they were and weren't like Henry. They gave advice to a peacock puppet, then traced their hands and colored in the peacock feathers.

The story is useful in individual or group therapy to help attention-seeking, emotionally needy clients learn other, more pro-social ways to relate to those around them.

THE PROUD PEACOCK

Henry, a young peacock that lived at the zoo, was a show-off, and sometimes he could be a real pain in the neck! One summer sunny day in June, Henry was strutting through the zoo to show off his colorful tail feathers. In case you wondered why he was strutting instead of just walking, Henry just LOVED showing off his highly colorful tail. He knew that other peacocks also had beautiful feathers, but he believed his were the brightest, longest, and most beautiful of all.

You know how people say, "ready, set, go," when they are playing a game? Well, Henry played "ready, set, go" with his feathers.

Henry would think, "Ready," as he stood tall and stared at someone in his path.

Once he got their attention, he would think, "Set," shaking his tail a little and making his feathers vibrate.

Finally, with a great "Ta-dah!" Henry would think, "Go!" and suddenly spread all his feathers out in a big ring around his body.

People went "Ooh!" and "Ah!" in an excited tone of voice when Henry spread his tail feathers. Henry just LOVED making them go "Ooh" and "Ah!" Henry also loved to listen to his own voice. When he saw people coming down the zoo path, he shouted loud enough to startle them (in peacock language): "*I'm* so handsome! I'm *so* clever! All the girl peacocks fall in love with me! All the people at the zoo admire me!"

Henry got jealous when he saw people paying attention to other animals at the zoo. He didn't like to share. When he saw people watching other animals, Henry did something to bring the attention back to himself, like crying out loudly or suddenly spreading his feathers.

When other animals saw him coming, they said, "Oh no, here comes that annoying big-mouth bird Henry again." They would roll their eyes and walk, swim, or fly away as quickly as possible, because they thought he was rude and selfish.

"Henry," they said, "you don't care about anyone but yourself!"

It was true—Henry loved himself better than anyone or anything else!

One day, Henry was in a very bad mood. "I need some attention *right now*," he thought. And because he was in a very bad mood, Henry wanted *all* the attention. And how would he do that?

Henry decided he would do three things to get *all* the attention. First, he would leave his tail feathers open all day long, to *make* everyone look at him. Next, he would shout loudly all day long, to *make* everyone listen to him. Last, he would follow people around to *make* everyone notice him. That would *surely* do the trick. So after a "ta-dah," Henry opened his feathers and started following people around. He cried out loudly.

At first, people went, "ooh" and "ah," but after a while he heard a man say, "There's that annoying, loud bird, again. Let's go see the elephants."

Next, he heard a woman say, "I wish that noisy bird would leave us alone. Let's go watch the monkeys." Even a child said, "He's so loud!" and covered his ears.

Henry tried harder and harder to get people's attention, but people took their children by the hands and walked away when they saw him coming. Henry saw a quiet female peacock resting by the path and said, "Excuse me. May I ask you a question?"

She replied, "I've been watching you strut around and make noise all day. So if you want to ask me a question, you better be ready for an honest answer."

Henry wasn't sure he was ready for an honest answer, but he asked his question anyway. "Why is everyone ignoring me today? I did everything I could think of to get *all* the attention. Instead, I'm getting *no* attention. Until today, everyone loved to watch me."

The female peacock replied, "Well, too much of a good thing is no longer a good thing. What you are doing now is selfish. You are not the only animal at the zoo. You are not the only peacock with beautiful feathers. If you want people to pay attention to you," added the female peacock, "you need to learn to share the spotlight with others."

According to his new friend, there were too many animals at the zoo for him to expect to get ALL the attention. And maybe if he learned to share, the other animals would not hate him so much. According to her, he might even make a friend or two.

Henry tried what the female peacock had suggested. He still acted like a peacock, but he did not demand constant attention. He stopped interrupting other animals, and he waited when it was their turn to have attention. The other animals stopped avoiding him so much, and he remembered to compliment other peacocks on their beautiful colors. Henry had found a good balance, even if he did sometimes still think he was the most beautiful peacock at the zoo!

THE BOTTOM LINE: Too much of a good thing is no longer a good thing.

2

Bullying and Anger Management

The Dragon's Fire

Children need to be able to regulate affect and express feelings appropriately. There are many types of children who bully others or have difficulty managing their anger: pre-teen boys wanting to be "tough" and masculine; children who witness domestic violence; children going through a difficult divorce at home; or even an over-indulged child who does not know how to get along with others. With cognitive behavioral treatment, motivational interviewing, proper mentoring, and encouragement, angry, bullying children can sometimes even be transformed into natural leaders. Without remediation, however, some angry children will not develop the capacity for empathy toward others, and more serious problems, such as conduct disorder, can emerge.

The young dragon in *The Dragon's Fire* is impressed with his own fire and uses it to *torment* others, which creates a rift between him and his peers. The story suggests that it is not anger that is bad; it is the way in which it is displayed in behavior. The bullying dragon in this story does not want to give up his fire power, since he would feel too vulnerable without it. It is important to note that the story's solution is not to take away the fire, to isolate/jail the dragon, to punish the dragon, to forcefully *make* the dragon stop, or to put the fire out. The story's solution is about balance and using one's own power in socially appropriate ways.

The story will lead nicely into interventions focused on self-control and the modulation of affect. Some children may wish to have a puppet show and help the dragon solve his problem. Other children may draw the dragon and talk about what in the child resembles the dragon's fire. Problem-solving about anger management, role-playing, and cost-benefit analysis (using vs. controlling fire) are helpful as well.

THE DRAGON'S FIRE

Once upon a time there was a young dragon that bullied everyone in the neighborhood. Flame may have been a young dragon, but he was bossy and had no friends. Every night he pounded his nasty feet on his scaly chest and shouted, "No one can beat me at anything—I'm king of the dragons!" Of course, he was not king. His uncle Smoky, a wise old dragon, was really the king. But the bossy young dragon liked to pretend he was king and scare all the people in the kingdom.

You may wonder how such a young dragon could scare an entire kingdom. Well, you see, Flame had a huge, ugly mouth full of sharp, nasty teeth, and when he roared, he spit out great balls of orange and red fire. When he opened his mouth, you could see all the way back to his tonsils, and you could smell his bad breath.

Flame loved to scare people with his fire—when he got mad, he would burn down a house or torch a tree. He burned a whole shopping mall one night after it had closed, in a fit of rage. Flame was proud of his power and strength. Even when he didn't burn things up, he made fun of others ("Nah, nah, nah-nah, nah!") and tried to scare them. He was a real bully. He threatened, "If you don't do what I want, I'll burn your house down." He always got his way, because everyone knew what a bad temper he had.

When other kid-dragons saw Flame coming, they ran away. No one wanted to play with him. You might be surprised, but once in a while Flame felt a little bit lonely. He thought, "No one will play with me—not even Jimmy the ugly troll! Not even the other bullies like me!" That was true—not even the bullies liked Flame, because he was the meanest, toughest bully of all.

One afternoon, Uncle Smoky came to visit Flame. Flame loved his uncle Smoky. Uncle Smoky played Dragon Ball with Flame, and he used his big blue spiked tail to send the ball flying. In case you did not know it, Dragon Ball is a game like dodgeball, using great balls of fire. But this visit was not to play Dragon Ball—Uncle Smoky had heard about his nephew's reputation as a bully. He said, "Flame, let's go eat at McDragon's and have ourselves a little talk." Once they got to McDragon's, Flame ordered a dragon-flamed burger and fries, and they squatted down on a long tree trunk bench to eat.

Then Uncle Smoky said, "Flame, I've been hearing some things about your reputation as a bully. What's up?"

"Yes," admitted Flame, "I am a bit of a bully. I have to admit that I kind of enjoy using my fire to scare people. I wouldn't mind having some friends, but I don't want to give up my fire."

Flame's uncle asked, "Exactly how do you use your fire now?" Flame told his uncle about what he did to scare people with his fire.

His uncle suggested, "The *way* you use your fire seems to be the problem. Dragon fire is for self-defense, not for picking on others. No one likes a bully!" His uncle added, kindly, "It is important to keep your fire—it helps you survive—but it is just as important to control it."

"What do you mean?" asked Flame.

His uncle replied, "When you control your fire, it is a good thing. When you don't control it, it is destructive."

His uncle continued, "So, Flame, tell me some good things about fire."

Flame thought for a minute and answered, "A dragon can blow a little fire as a warning to scare off a dangerous giant."

"Good thinking," said his uncle.

Flame added, "And we also need fire to cook or keep us warm."

Flame's uncle questioned, "Now how can fire be bad?"

Flame said, "That's easy—it can quickly get out of control and damage or destroy things it touches." He added, "It can also burn and cause pain."

"That's right," said Uncle Smoky, as he scratched his scaly back with his back claws. "Those are ways that fire can hurt. If you want to make friends, you need to stop being a bully. Use your fire in ways that help, not hurt."

Flame decided to try to control his fire and be less of a bully. He thought that Dragon School would be a good place to start. In case you did not know it, Dragon School is where dragons learn to blow smoke rings and write messages with smoke letters. During recess, they throw fireballs at targets and play Dragon Ball.

During recess the next day, Flame went up to a group of young dragons and said, "Can I play with you?" They looked scared and flew off in the other direction before Flame could tell them he was sorry for being a bully and that he wanted to change.

After school, Flame flew into town, and as he approached McDragon's, he called out, "Anyone want to play Dragon Ball later?" Everyone ran off when they saw Flame—there was no way they would come near him, because they didn't trust him. Who wants to get torched?

Then Flame saw his uncle across the street and shouted, "Uncle Smoky, could you help me convince the people that I want to change?"

Uncle Smoky suggested that Flame might do something nice for the town, to show them some new behavior. So from 50 yards away, Flame called out, "This Saturday, I'm planning a little flight over the forest and across the mountains. Come let me take you for a ride on my back. I'll show you sights you have never seen. I *promise* I won't hurt you!"

Uncle Smoky talked to the frightened people and told them that Flame had "turned over a new leaf." He promised that they would be safe, and he said he would join them on the flight. They trusted Flame's uncle Smoky and agreed to give Flame a chance.

That Saturday, about 50 people climbed on Flame's large scaly back, and Flame's uncle flew ahead as the leader. "Follow me!" he called out. The people held on to Flame's spiny plates as he took off going about 50 miles per hour. "Hold on tight!" Flame cried. Up, up into the sky he flew! Flame flew toward some thick clouds. "Whoosh!" went Flame's hot breath as he blew the clouds away. When people got a little chilly, Flame blew out a little fire to warm the air around them. They traveled over the mountain, looked down on the blue lakes and green valleys below, and then landed to have a wonderful picnic. They found the perfect spot to have a campfire, one that would not create a forest fire.

The young dragon shouted, "And now, my wonderful new friends, I will show off my fire!" As they watched in amazement, he opened his huge mouth and spit out a ball of orange and red fire, *away* from all the people. Then Flame used his fire to light a lovely campfire. The people put hot dogs and marshmallows on *long* sticks, and the dragon cooked them to perfection. Everyone had a wonderful time, once they got over their fear that he might roast *them*. They all agreed that it had been a magical, exciting day.

When Flame returned to Dragon School on Monday, one of the young dragons invited him to play Dragon Ball at recess. The dragons had heard about Flame turning over a new leaf. From that day on, Flame began to make friends, and he kept his promise not to be a bully.

Flame was proud of his decision to change, and he continued to control his fire. Once in a while, he showed off his fire, but he was careful to not scare or hurt anyone. When he got in a really bad mood and felt like torching someone (because no one is perfect and everyone gets in a bad mood sometimes), he went flying by himself until he felt better. Sort of the dragon version of *time-out*! Flame had learned to have his fire and control it, too!

THE BOTTOM LINE: Have your fire and control it, too!

3

Unconditional Positive Self-Regard

The Unraveled Tapestry

Children, particularly girls as they approach adolescence, may become self-critical and begin to view themselves as "not good enough." Low self-esteem may result in children or teens splitting off parts of the self that they judge to be unacceptable. In addition, when children go through difficult times and lack resilience to cope well with changes, stress may become a risk factor for later pathology.

The following story, *The Unraveled Tapestry*, is about a child gaining self-acceptance through the unconditional positive regard of a caring adult. In this story, the unconditional positive regard is provided by a parent, but for other children, it might need to be a therapist, or youth worker, or even a teacher. Children need adults to love them "just the way they are" and to help them feel acceptable as whole human beings.

Children that receive excess criticism, teasing, bullying, or judgment from others as well as children and teens that expect perfection in themselves have difficulty constructing a strong, positive sense of self. They need adults to help them figure out how to maintain a positive sense of self in the midst of a challenging peer culture by maximizing their strengths.

Therapists can help children and teens integrate the "good me" and "bad me" parts, or even, in some children, the "me" and "not me" parts of the self. This story is helpful when read with a child as well as with the child's parents, as parents contribute a great deal toward a child's self-evaluation.

THE UNRAVELED TAPESTRY

Donna Weaver was lying on her purple-and-green-colored comforter in her purple-and-green-colored bedroom, staring at the bright purple walls, deep in thought. Donna really liked the color purple, and whenever she wanted to get away from it all, she went into her bedroom, shut the door, and wrote in her journal or listened to music.

That day, as Donna stared at her walls and listened to music, her eyes were drawn to a woven tapestry on her wall, as if there was a strong magnet in the tapestry and she was a magnetic object! Donna looked closely at the tapestry.

She spoke. "I have had that thing hanging on my wall since the day I was born, and it is one of the ugliest things I have ever seen."

Donna was exaggerating a bit, since the tapestry was unusual looking, but not really ugly. It was woven with threads and materials of all types and colors. It had texture to it and quite a bit of character. It had a personality all its own, and the colors and fabrics sort of fit together. You might have heard the saying, "The whole is greater than the sum of its parts." Well, the tapestry was like that. Each separate thread was not much to look at, but together the threads made a nice sort of whole.

Some of the tapestry threads were rough and some were smooth. There was silk, and rope, and plastic cord, and pot holder loops, and strips of cloth, and even pieces of clean, white baby diapers. There were woven threads of black wire, and pink yarn, and computer power supply cords. There were shiny brocade fabrics and red corduroy as well as blue denim and sheer curtains.

Donna liked the brocade and corduroy, but she hated some of the other threads. And she didn't have much say about it. The tapestry was a self-weaving one. It was born the day Donna was born and every time something important happened to her, another thread was woven in. The tapestry had a thread in it for every part of Donna and her life.

Donna had an idea. She would just take out the threads she did not like—remove the ones that bothered her or reminded her of *bad* memories. The first thread Donna pulled out was the one made of gauze bandage. It had been woven in the time she had to get stitches in her forehead after falling on the playground. She didn't want to remember that! Then she took out the thread from the dress she wore the Christmas her parents got divorced. She also decided to remove the shoelace from her first-grade tennis shoe—Jimmy had teased her about those tennis shoes and made her cry. Forget that!

So Donna unwove the tapestry, one *bad* thread at a time, until there was a pile of unwanted threads sitting on the floor of her bedroom. She hung what remained of the tapestry back on her bedroom wall and hid the *extra* threads way in the back of her bedroom closet.

Now, the tapestry looked even more unusual. There were big gaps in the threads. The wall showed through the gaps and the purple color did not go with the threads that were left. The loose threads of the tapestry slumped and stuck out away from the wall. But Donna didn't care. She had finally gotten rid of the pieces she didn't like.

A couple of days later, while Donna was daydreaming in her bedroom, she heard a knock on her door.

"Who is it?" Donna called out.

"It's me," said her mom with a smile in her voice. "I have some of your laundry to put away. Can I come in?"

"Sure," said Donna.

Donna's mom came in and started putting away clothes in Donna's drawers. Then, she stopped suddenly and stared at Donna's wall where the tapestry was hanging. Her mouth hung open with surprise.

"What happened to your tapestry?" asked Mom, and the smile in her voice was gone.

Donna thought, "Oh-oh. I think she notices what I did to the tapestry." Donna decided to act real casual and innocent, as if nothing had happened.

"What's up, Mom?" asked Donna.

"Donna," replied her mother, "you *know* what I'm talking about. What happened to your tapestry? It looks awful."

"What do you mean?" asked Donna, still trying to act innocent.

Her mother looked her straight in the eye. "Come on, Donna. Tell me the truth. What did you do to the tapestry? Pieces of it are missing. It isn't complete anymore."

"Oh, Mom," said Donna. "Don't make such a big deal out of it. I fixed it. I took out the parts I didn't like and put them away. I want to forget about those parts."

Donna's mother disagreed. "It was beautiful just the way it was. The tapestry was born when you were born and it held the memories of your life. It isn't whole without the other threads, and you aren't whole without those parts of your life."

"Well, I kept the best parts, the ones that are special to me," said Donna.

Her mother replied, "Every part of it was special to me, just as every part of you is special to me. Now it has unraveled and is falling apart. It's no longer whole."

"I don't want the *bad* parts in there," argued Donna. "When I look at it on my wall, I don't want to see the *bad* memories."

"Donna," her mother said kindly and very gently, "we all go through *good* and *bad* times. You might have never noticed, but the threads you put away added contrast to the tapestry. The beauty of the brighter threads is more noticeable when you see them next to the dark ones. The *bad* threads add strength and help hold the tapestry together. You need to *keep the bad with the good*. And remember, there is nothing *bad* about you. At least think about it . . ."

They said goodnight, and Donna thought awhile about what her mother had said. She stared carefully at the tapestry on her wall. She had not noticed it before, but the pretty threads still on the tapestry were too much alike. They were made of bright-colored, smooth materials. They had little depth and did not hold together well. They were drooping and unraveling without the darker threads to hold them in place. No two threads hidden in her closet were alike, and many had interesting stories to tell.

Donna had a sudden *aha*. "I am a weaver!" she realized. "I can reweave my tapestry!"

Donna went to her closet and pulled out the pile of tangled, darker threads. She wove them back into the tapestry, using a new pattern of her own creation, so that the tapestry had a whole new look. When she finished, Donna hung the tapestry back on her wall.

Donna stared at the tapestry and thought, "The new tapestry is more beautiful than the original one. The threads are holding together better. I don't know how that happened. I used the same old threads, but I rearranged them a bit and ended up with a truly lovely creation."

It was true. The dark, coarse threads contrasted with the brighter colors and the varied textures made it a thing of beauty, whole and complete. There were no more unraveling threads, and somehow everything fit together.

THE BOTTOM LINE: Every thread counts!

4

Codependency

Enough Is Enough

Some children learn from their parents to be what many writers have labeled *codependent.* They take care of or help others at their own expense. It is not a bad thing to help others; but it is not good to ignore or minimize one's own needs. It is also not a good thing to allow others to walk all over, take advantage of, or put down one's own self. In families with substance abuse or domestic violence, for example, persons' needs/rights are violated or ignored. It is good for children to realize that each person in a family is worth being the recipient of tender, loving care. It is also good to explicitly state that it is OK to value yourself as much as you do others, but not more or less than.

Mothers that allow their partners to mistreat them in front of the children in order to "be nice" or "not make waves" send a negative message about relationships and put their children at risk. Men sponsoring others in AA at the expense of family time need to realize that healthy, strong family relationships are part of recovery.

Samantha Sheep is a very kind, caring friend. Unfortunately she carries it a little too far and needs to be reminded that she has needs of her own. Family members can discuss who they resemble most in the story or nominate others in the family for the parts of Samantha and her friends. Children can give advice to Samantha and then discuss how they let their friends "walk all over" them or, conversely, take advantage of others. Children will enjoy reading this story and relating it to their own lives.

ENOUGH IS ENOUGH

Samantha Sheep heard a loud voice calling from across the pasture. It was her friend Pig. "Black sheep, black sheep, have you any wool?" Samantha called back, in an annoyed voice, "Go away and leave me alone!" She sounded very upset.

"Now wait a minute," you say. I suspect that you know the next line of this nursery rhyme is not supposed to be, "Go away and leave me alone." The next line is supposed to be, "Yes, sir, yes, sir, three bags full." So you might ask, "What is going on with Samantha Sheep?" And I might answer, "Sit down and relax, and I'll tell you."

Samantha was a sweet, kind, and generous sheep. She almost never talked to anyone in an annoyed voice. She had a big heart and gave freely of herself, even the wool off her back. She liked to do things to please others and make them happy. But this day, Samantha had a reason to be upset. She was naked and cold, and her breath came out like a foggy cloud as it hit the chilly air.

You might wonder why Samantha Sheep was naked and shivering in the cold on a sunny spring day. After all, a sheep is an animal that usually has plenty of soft, warm wool on its back. Poor Samantha. She was too kind for her own good. On Monday, her friend Barn Cat came to see her and meowed, "Black sheep, black sheep, have you any wool?"

Samantha smiled and replied, 'Yes, cat, yes, cat, three bags full."

"Oh, good!" said Barn Cat. "I want to make a lovely black wool hat to warm my ears when I sleep in the barn on cold spring nights."

Then Samantha sheared some wool off her back to give to Barn Cat so that she could make her hat. In case you did not know, "sheared" is a word that means to cut off the sheep's wool. It doesn't hurt when a sheep is sheared. The wool covering the sheep's body is clipped off (a little like a haircut), and later it grows back.

"Thank you for the wool!" purred Barn Cat as she ran back to the barn, twitching her tail. "You are a kind and generous friend."

That night, Samantha felt the cold wind blowing on her bare back and was glad she still had the rest of her wool to keep her warm. "It's good to share my wool," she thought. "I am a little chilly tonight, but my wool will grow back soon."

On Tuesday, her friend Watch Dog came to see her and barked, "Black sheep, black sheep, have you any wool?"

Samantha smiled and replied, "Yes, dog, yes, dog, three bags full."

"Oh good," said Watch Dog. "I want to make a black wool sweater to warm my back in the cold spring air."

Then Samantha sheared off the rest of the wool on her back, which was enough wool to make the dog's sweater.

"Thank you so much," barked Watch Dog as he ran off to protect the farm. "You are a kind and generous friend."

That night, the cold wind numbed Samantha's totally bare back. She curled up next to another sheep in the pasture to keep warm. Her teeth were chattering and she shivered all night.

Samantha thought, "I'm very cold tonight, but I don't want to complain. It is good to share my wool with others. My wool will grow back soon."

On Wednesday, her friend Milk Cow came to see Samantha and mooed, "Black sheep, black sheep, have you any wool?"

Samantha bleated, "Yes, cow, yes, cow, three bags full."

"Oh, good!" said Milk Cow. "I would like to make a long, black wool scarf to wear around my neck. It would look lovely with my black and white spots, and it will warm my neck on cold spring nights."

"You will look lovely wearing a long black scarf," agreed Samantha. Then Samantha sheared the wool off her belly, head, and rump so that Milk Cow could have her scarf.

Milk Cow said, "You are a kind and generous friend!" as she waddled back to the barn.

That night Samantha bleated in distress. She was totally naked and had nothing to keep her warm in the cold spring air.

"I hope I don't freeze to death," thought Samantha as a tear fell from her eye. "I have no more wool on my body. I know it will grow back in time, but that thought will not help me on this cold, spring night."

Poor Samantha did not sleep at all that night as she huddled with the other sheep in the pasture.

So now you understand why Samantha spoke to Pig in an annoyed voice the next morning when he came to ask her for some wool. But the minute Samantha said, "Go away and leave me alone!" she felt a little guilty. She really liked to be generous and give the wool off her back to her friends. She enjoyed pleasing them and making them happy. Samantha felt sad that she had nothing left to give.

And then her friend Pig did something that surprised Samantha. Pig walked over to her in the pasture and said kindly, "Why are you standing naked in the cold spring air? What has happened to all your wool?"

Samantha replied, "I gave my friends all the wool off my back. I like to please them and make them happy."

Pig said, "Enough is enough! It's wonderful to have friends and to do things to make them happy, but you need to keep some of your wool for yourself. You won't be much help to your friends if you end up frozen like a block of ice!"

He added, "Sometimes you have to take care of yourself before you take care of others."

Pig gave a loud "OINK" that could be heard all the way to the barn, and he shouted, "Barn Cat, Watch Dog, and Milk Cow, please come out to the pasture."

Out of the barn came the cat, the dog, and the cow. Barn Cat was purring and wearing a lovely black wool hat. Watch Dog was panting happily, sporting a handsome black wool sweater. And Milk Cow gave a loud "Moo" as she showed off her long, black wool scarf. They wondered why Pig had called them out of the barn. They were afraid he might be charging them a fine for leaving such a "smelly mess" on the barnyard floor. Pig was the newly elected president of the Barnyard Association.

Then they saw their shivering friend Samantha standing in the pasture with Pig, and all three came running over.

"Samantha," meowed Barn Cat, "you are naked and have nothing to warm your head. You must borrow my wool hat!" And with that, Barn Cat put the hat on Samantha's head.

"Samantha," barked Watch Dog, "your back is bare and the air is cold. You must borrow my sweater." And with that, Watch Dog draped his new sweater over Samantha's shivering back.

Milk Cow mooed, "Samantha, you must borrow my scarf. It will warm your neck when the cold spring wind is blowing." And with that, Milk Cow wrapped her long, black scarf around Samantha's sheared neck.

"We're sorry," said Samantha's friends. "We didn't realize that you gave us all the wool off your back, neck, head, and belly. Please wear the hat, sweater, and scarf until your wool grows back."

Samantha smiled at her friends. "You are such good friends," she bleated. "Soon, my wool will grow back, and then I will return the hat, the sweater, and the scarf. Next time I'll keep a little wool for myself."

Samantha's friends headed back to the barn to clean up the "dirty mess" to avoid getting a fine. They drew straws to see which one would get the "dirtiest job" of bagging the "poop."

From that day forward, Samantha took good care of herself. She was still a kind and generous sheep, but after all, no one is expected to give ALL the wool off his or her back.

THE BOTTOM LINE: Enough is enough!

5

Planning Ahead (Executive Functioning)

Steer Clear of the Rocks

Children with sequencing or executive functioning deficits have problems with organization and planning ahead. They have trouble *connecting the dots* in their daily lives; indeed, at times they don't see the dots. When they do see the dots, they don't see any order to them and respond in a trial-and-error or impulsive, poorly planned manner.

As a result, some children with executive functioning difficulties take undue risks. These children are like magnets drawn to unsafe situations. They seek high levels of arousal and do not evaluate their environment for persons or things that might result in harm. You might call them injury or accident prone. Their lives are a series of *oops*, and the *aha*, if it comes, comes after the fact. They may regret getting hurt or hurting others, but they don't see it coming beforehand.

Another area of life affected by executive functioning deficits is social interaction. For relationships to work, children need to be able to sequence and engage in the *back-and-forth* aspects of communication. These children jump right in and say whatever is on their minds without noticing the sequence or the overall flow of the conversation. They offend others without intending to and are unable to see themselves as others see them.

Many children with executive functioning deficits have academic difficulties. When presenting in class, they jump around and have trouble sticking to an outline. As a result, their presentations appear quite disorganized. When writing, they have difficulty organizing facts into a cohesive whole. Such children do not filter out irrelevant details, and *they lose the forest for the trees*.

This story introduces the concepts of attending to environmental details, sequencing, and doing things in a reasonable order. CBT games and interventions are a logical next step.

STEER CLEAR OF THE ROCKS

Olivia Otter had a *slight problem*. She lived in Myrtle Beach, South Carolina, and her friend Jenny had asked her to go swimming. Olivia had to figure out how to explain to Jenny why she couldn't go with her to the beach that afternoon, even though she loved to swim. It was a little embarrassing. Her right big toe was bandaged from where the large crab in the ocean had pinched it with its claw. Her left ankle was still healing from the jellyfish sting. Her right arm was going to be in the pink cast another 3 weeks from falling in the water while white-water rafting in West Virginia. And the stitches in her forehead (from her fall as she crossed the creek on the stepping-stones) were due to come out in 7 days.

She must be very unlucky, you say? Well, it was more than bad luck. Olivia had trouble *noticing and avoiding things* that could hurt her. She was a fun-loving otter that craved excitement. She wasn't afraid of anything! She went on every roller coaster in every park, loved hang-gliding over the ocean, and did the bungee jumping at the state fair. She went white-water rafting and snorkeling in Florida every summer. She wanted to take scuba diving lessons next, but her mother said, "No," because she was afraid Olivia would forget to fill her oxygen tank or to turn it on.

That was part of the problem. Olivia forgot to plan ahead. She was very brave and fun loving but she didn't pay attention to details. For example, one time she packed a parachute in the wrong way and it was all tangled up. Fortunately, the instructor checked it and helped her re-pack it. If she had jumped with that parachute, she could have been killed!

It is one thing to have an accident. But it is another thing to have an accident because you were not careful and could have prevented it or seen it coming.

"Ding-dong" went her doorbell. Olivia went to open the door. There was her friend Jenny.

Jenny took one look at Olivia and said, "Uh, I guess we won't be going swimming today. I came over to see why you didn't return my phone call." She tried not to look shocked at her friend's bandages, cast, and stitches. She waited for Olivia to tell her what happened.

Olivia said, smiling, "Don't worry, Jenny. It looks bad, but it hardly hurts at all. I can't go swimming today but soon everything will heal and I'll be back in the water."

Jenny couldn't wait any longer to ask. "What happened to you?"

"Just a few strokes of bad luck," replied Olivia.

Olivia began to tell Jenny the stories of her various accidents.

"First," she said, "you know that creek we like to wade in? I missed a few of the stepping-stones when I tried to jump from the first one to the fifth. It didn't work—I fell and hit my head on a rock. That's how I got the stitches in my forehead.

"Next, I went to the beach and didn't notice the sign warning people to stay out of the water due to lots of jellyfish that day. I went in anyway and got stung 5 times on my ankle. It's OK—I applied meat tenderizer and used my mom's credit card to scrape off the stingers.

"A week after that, I went white-water rafting. You know how I love the thrill of those big waves! Well, our guide told us to paddle to the left around a huge rock and I decided to go right over it instead. My raft capsized (tipped over) and I broke my arm."

She added, "I couldn't avoid the crab. By the time I saw it, it was too late."

Jenny was a very honest friend. She said, "You know, it's not so much bad luck as it is you not being careful."

She continued, "You can have lots of excitement and be careful at the same time. You just need to do things in order, follow directions, and plan ahead."

"Yeah, I know," said Olivia. "But that's really hard to do."

Jenny suggested "It's not hard when you plan what you're going to do. For example, when we cross the creek, while your feet are still secure on the rocks, look ahead for the next rock. Find one close to your front foot that's not too slippery and move your foot. Walk through the creek one rock at a time. You can even test the rocks to make sure they won't wobble. Then you won't fall."

"I don't mind falling and getting wet," said Olivia. "I'm an otter, after all. But I don't want to fall and get hurt. I think I'll try that the next time we walk in the creek."

Then Jenny said, "Before you go swimming, check the warnings and posted signs. We live right near the beach. If the water conditions aren't safe, we can wait and swim another day. It's better to be safe than sorry."

"I know," Olivia agreed. "Jellyfish stings are something I could live without."

Olivia added, "I guess I wasn't thinking very clearly when I went over the rock in the raft."

"White-water rafting requires planning ahead," said Jenny. "It's a great sport and very exciting. But there's lots of danger, too. You have to look way ahead on the river to find rocks and steer around them. Always steer around the rocks—don't try to go over them."

Jenny and Olivia decided to put a jigsaw puzzle together that afternoon out on the patio. Olivia wanted to go Rollerblading but Jenny thought it would not be safe with Olivia in a cast. It would probably take

Olivia some time to learn how to plan ahead and quit getting hurt. She figured she could ask Jenny's advice when her own judgment might be a little off. After all, it is a good thing to want fun and excitement in your life, but you don't want to get hurt in the process!

THE BOTTOM LINE: Steer clear of the rocks!

6

Recognizing Positives

Treasures in the Trash

It takes a couple of smart rats in *Treasures in the Trash* to help the townspeople realize that their black and white, rigid thinking prevents them from noticing *treasures* of value. The main point of this story is that negative attitudes can lead to undue focus on the negative aspects of life.

Some children and teens in treatment are notorious for all-or-nothing thinking, and they inevitably see the glass as *half-empty*. They complain, criticize, and judge with their negative slant on life and will need help if they are to change their *always* and *nevers* to a more balanced view of the world.

Problem-solving and decision-making require flexible thinking. In the vein of positive psychology (Seligman and Csikszentmihalyi) this story may be used to help individuals attend to the positive aspects of their lives.

Children in therapy will enjoy hearing how the rats help the townspeople gain a more balanced view of their *garbage*, and it is an easy jump to take them on a *treasure hunt* to relate the story to their own thoughts and perceptions, their own *treasures* and *trash*.

TREASURES IN THE TRASH

Roland, a big fat gray and white rat, had chewed his way through the plastic trash bag and was hungrily eating everything in sight. Roland Rat had invited Rachael, his white-furred friend, to join him for "A Taste of the Town" at the local garbage dump, located a few miles outside the small town of Toss-It-All.

"Come here, Rachael," Roland called out with excitement. "This bag has leftover Caesar salad, hot dogs, and PB and J sandwiches."

Rachael scurried over to join him, and soon her furry white coat was spotted with ketchup, mustard, and blackberry jelly. Roland had a big grin on his fat furry face, and there was a piece of brown, slimy lettuce hanging out of his mouth.

"Mmm, mmm," said Roland. "This garbage is absolutely delicious!"

The small houses in Toss-It-All were painted black with white shutters. The people in the town wore black and white clothes and drove black and white cars. The town had a big black and white wall around it—no one could see outside the town limits, and no one traveled outside the town limits. Some of the people had lived so long in the town of Toss-It-All that they forgot the rest of the world existed! As the rats ate their way through blackened banana peels, bluish green pieces of moldy bread, smelly steak bones, and rotten lettuce, they smacked their lips and exclaimed, "Delicious! Delectable! Delightful!" You know, only a rat can appreciate the finer aspects of rotting garbage.

Then, as Roland pushed his pointy nose deep into the trash bag, he crunched down with his teeth on something hard. "Ouch!" he said with disgust. "There are things in this garbage that don't belong here—I'm going to break a tooth if I'm not careful!"

Roland stopped eating for a moment as he spit out the hard thing that was in his mouth, and then he resumed eating the tasty garbage. He was too hungry to let a few hard objects get between the garbage and his stomach. After all, he LOVED to eat!

For the rest of the day, Roland and Rachael continued munching on piles of delectable garbage, and they continued to find hard, inedible objects in the trash. In case you did not know it, "inedible" means things that you are not supposed to eat.

Eat—crunch—spit. Eat—crunch—spit.

Before long, there was a small pile of inedible objects that each of them had spit out, rather than break a tooth. It was a very unusual pile of objects. To begin with, there were several sparkling nuggets of gold. There were also 10 smooth pearls and 5 small black rocks.

If you looked really closely, you could see that the black rocks were diamonds in the rough—"rough" means that they weren't cut or polished yet so they weren't sparkly or clear. They looked like worthless black lumps, but they were diamonds just the same. They just needed a bit of work.

Roland said, "What a waste to put these things in the trash. These things are no use to rats but very valuable to humans. Why did they throw them out?"

Rachael replied, "When garbage day comes, the people of Toss-It-All toss everything in their trash. They throw out the good with the bad, trash and treasures. I don't think they know the difference between trash and treasures. Or maybe they just don't take the time to sort the treasures from the trash before they throw out their garbage."

"Well," said Roland, "Let's attend the next Toss-It-All town meeting and remind the people not to put these things in our trash. I don't want to chip a tooth just because they won't sort the treasures from the trash."

And so it was that Roland and Rachael went to speak at the next Toss-It-All town meeting. On the night of the meeting, Roland and Rachael Rat showed up right on time. They went up to the front of the room and perched up on top of the podium so that they could be heard in the microphone.

Roland, his little nose twitching, squeaked, "Ladies and gentlemen, we are here to complain about how you throw away your trash." Roland continued. "When we went to the dump last week, I almost chipped my tooth. Rachael and I found many things in your trash that don't belong there and are valuable to humans. We suggest that you look through your garbage a bit more closely. If you sort the treasures from the trash before it is brought to the dump, then we won't chip our teeth."

Many people asked questions and talked with the rats about the problem. One person admitted, "We are very busy black and white people living in a black and white town. But we don't mean to throw away treasures. Can you show us some of the things you found?"

Roland agreed. "I brought some of the treasures with me so that you could see what we found." He showed them the gold and the pearls, and everyone said, "Ooh!" and "Ah!" They could not believe that those things were mixed in with the trash at the garbage dump.

But when he pulled out the uncut diamonds, someone said, "Now those are uncut diamonds. They are hard to recognize, so you have to look even more closely to find them." (In case you did not know it, the word "recognize" means to see something and know what it is.) "When you take the time to cut and polish uncut diamonds, they go from black lumps to clear, sparkling gems. They are valuable treasures!"

The Toss-It-All townspeople realized they had stopped paying attention to what they threw away and what they kept. So from that day on, they all worked harder to sort the good from the bad, the treasures from the trash. They learned that with a little effort, they could pay attention to the valuable things in their lives, even the uncut diamonds that were harder to spot. It's amazing what you can discover when you are looking carefully.

Someone proposed changing the name of the town to "Toss-Only-the-Trash," but the vote was 60–40, with 60 people against it. That is not surprising, for as you know, change takes time and you need to change things one small step at a time.

THE BOTTOM LINE: Separate treasures from the trash.

7

Intolerance and Prejudice

The Brown-Eyed Club

In 1968, Jane Elliott was just another American third and fourth grade school teacher at a school in Riceville, Iowa, an all-white small American town. On April 5, 1968, she used a "blue-eyed/brown-eyed exercise" to introduce her students to the idea of racial equality. The *Brown-Eyed Club* story that follows parallels the theme of the Jane Elliott classroom intervention.

The *Brown-Eyed Club* takes a poke at prejudice and intolerance. Young children are remarkably and wonderfully accepting toward other children. I still remember our then 3-year-old daughter's delight when she came home from preschool and asked if we had noticed what a beautiful brown face her teacher had. We told her that we had noticed. She said that she wished she had a beautiful brown face, since *plain white* was more boring.

As children grow older, they become less accepting of others and *us-them* cliques begin to exclude and judge those that are different. This makes life untenable for those who are a little heavier, cognitively slower, darker-in-skin, shyer, or just *weirder* than mainstream 11- to 13-year-olds. The social pecking order allows those *at the top* to feel and act superior toward those *below*.

In therapy, especially in group, it is very helpful to plant seeds with children about accepting those that are different. Differences may be race, ethnicity, or other cultural diversity areas, including rural/urban, religious/agnostic, Democrat/Republican, educated/dropout, or wealthy/poor. This story challenges *earthly prejudices* and provides good material for group discussion.

THE BROWN-EYED CLUB

Once upon a time, there was a happy and peaceful world known as the Land of Wun. The people that lived in the Land of Wun (better known as Wunians) were of all shapes and sizes.

In addition to being all shapes and sizes, Wunians had very unusual outside coverings. In our world we call it "skin" but in their world it did not look much like the skin we know. For example, some Wunians were covered with rough bark. Others had skin that crinkled like cellophane, and believe it or not, some Wunians were covered in sandpaper. One very cute three-eyed Wunian was coated in green slippery slime. The inhabitants of the Land of Wun all got along quite well and didn't pay much attention to their differences. Of course the Wunians with sandpaper "skin" kept their distance so no one would get "roughed up"!

In about the trillionth year of their world's existence, the Land of Wun had a series of unfortunate events. There was a water shortage and everyone got very thirsty. Then the climate changed, and everyone got quite chilly. There were not enough blankets to go around and they had to ration water. Stress, unknown in years past, was rising in the Land of Wun.

Then one day, a round-faced yellow Wunian said to a metal-covered friend, "You know, I just noticed that our eyes are not the same color. My eyes are brown and yours are blue. Please don't take it personally, but I think my brown eyes are more beautiful than your blue ones."

"What are you talking about?" questioned the friend. "My blue eyes are just as beautiful as your brown eyes."

"No," said the brown-eyed Wunian in a not-so-nice voice. "They aren't. It is as clear as the ugly blue eyes on your face. Brown eyes are better."

Ugly? Until that moment, no Wunian had ever been so unkind to a fellow Wunian! In fact, no Wunian had ever paid any attention to eye color at all. People in the Land of Wun had brown, black, pink, blue, green, and purple eyes. Until now, no one had really noticed or cared.

The blue-eyed Wunian walked off in a huff with her feelings hurt. She didn't like being treated that way by her friend. She told her family and friends what had happened, looking for sympathy, but there was very little agreement among them. Some thought that green eyes made you look smarter. Some thought that blue eyes made you look more kind. Others agreed with the brown-eyed Wunian that brown eyes were more beautiful.

Before long, the whole Land of Wun was arguing over eye color, and friends and neighbors were fussing as they never had before.

The next day, the brown-eyed Wunian decided to call a meeting of other brown-eyed Wunians. Hundreds of brown-eyed Wunians lined up at the door. Some blue-eyed Wunians who tried to enter were blocked from doing so. "You BLUE-EYED Wunian, go away. We don't want you here. This is OUR meeting!"

The brown-eyed leader called the meeting to order and passed out handouts to those in attendance. The handouts listed "facts" that "proved" brown-eyed Wunians were superior to blue-eyed Wunians. There were more brown-eyed Wunians than blue-eyed Wunians, for one thing. Second, blue-eyed Wunians were hardly ever elected to office, and not as many graduated from high school or college.

The "facts" indicated clearly that brown-eyed Wunians were smarter, richer, and more talented than others in the Land of Wun. At the end of the meeting, the brown-eyed Wunians voted to start the Brown-Eyed Club, and they agreed that other-eyed persons were not welcome.

The news of the meeting spread, and one thing led to another. Before long, there were brown-eyed neighborhoods, brown-eyed busses, brown-eyed restaurants, and brown-eyed schools. Brown-eyed Wunians picked on blue-eyed Wunians, calling them names and refusing to play or work with them. Wun was no longer a happy, peaceful place.

One day, an astronaut from Planet Earth came to visit the Land of Wun. A brown-eyed Wunian invited the Earthling to be a guest speaker at the Brown-Eyed Club. The Earthling told the Wunians about Earth's many years of conflict over skin color. The astronaut explained that hatred and stereotypes fueled the conflict on Earth, and that in spite of some very strong peacemaking efforts, the conflict continued.

"You ridiculous Earth people," laughed the brown-eyed Wunians. "Skin color is just the outer packaging—it means nothing at all. Now, eye color, that's another matter completely!"

The brown-eyed Wunians were now confident, as well, of their superiority over Earthlings. After all, who of any intelligence would fight over such a silly thing as skin color?

"You know," the Wunians said to the Earthling, "if you ever come to live in Wun, you'll have to live in the blue-eyed neighborhood. No brown-eyed Wunian in his or her right mind would want an Earthling as a neighbor, that's for sure."

THE BOTTOM LINE: Beauty is in the eye of the beholder (i.e., the Wun who beholds it!).

8

Inflexibility

Gold in the Desert

The miner in *Gold in the Desert* works very hard but accomplishes very little. His inflexibility blocks him from reaching his goal and he is ultimately unsuccessful.

The metaphor in this story is that people sometimes look for things in the wrong places or exhibit behaviors that are at odds with their goals. Often our clients *beat their heads against brick walls* or *try to squeeze water out of a rock*. They try to change things that can't be changed and end up frustrated. The Serenity Prayer of AA points out that we need to have the wisdom to recognize what can and can't be changed and then respond accordingly.

The little girl in this story points out that the man needs to either stay where he is and set new goals, or he needs to move in a new direction. It is a choice. Clients may forget that they have choices and feel *trapped* by life circumstances. This story will help them view their situations differently and consider whether or not to *make a move*.

Children of all ages get frustrated when they fail in their efforts. The story points out that it is important to look at your goals realistically and be flexible in your efforts if you are to be successful.

GOLD IN THE DESERT

Once upon a time, a girl was taking a walk in the desert, just down the road from her house. Have you ever seen a desert? Deserts are dry, bare, and flat as far as the eye can see. The hot sun glared down from high in the sky. Everything was dusty, and fine grains of sand kept getting into the girl's shoes. The heat made waves in the hazy, hot air, and off in the distance you could see the faint outline of a range of tall, snow-topped mountains. No one lived near the girl—her house was "out in the middle of nowhere" according to her friends.

As the girl walked, she took a drink from her water bottle and put some more sunscreen on her face and arms. Then suddenly the girl heard a loud voice: "Oh, *crap*!" The voice came from a tall man who was kneeling in the sand a few feet in front of her. Sweat was pouring down his red face as he scooped up some sand and sifted through it with a flat pan. The pan had very tiny holes in it and sand poured through them.

As the girl watched, the man threw down his sifter and said, again, very loudly, "Oh, *crap*!!!"

The girl giggled to herself. Everyone knew that "*crap*" was a *bad word* and not a nice thing to say. "I must be doing something wrong," said the red-faced man.

The girl was very curious and could not figure out what the man was doing. "Excuse me, mister," the girl said as she approached. "What are you trying to do?"

"That's obvious," he said. "I want to be a miner, and I'm searching for gold. I've sifted sand all day and haven't found *any* gold. I'm starting to get very upset. I've always been told that if you believe in yourself and work hard, you will be successful."

The girl thought, "He is one strange man! Everyone knows you sift for gold in a stream or mine gold up in the mountains. There is no water here, and the mountains are miles away."

The girl said, "I can tell that you have been working hard—your face is all red and you are covered in sand!"

Then the man said, "I feel like a failure, because I haven't found any gold. I must be doing something wrong."

The girl replied, trying to not hurt his feelings, "Mister, you're not doing anything wrong, but there is no gold here. Never has been—never will be. You might find gold up in the mountains. You're using the right tools—you're just looking in the wrong place."

"What do you mean?" asked the man.

"You could use that pan to sift through the sand in a stream up near the mountains," the girl answered. "If you want to find gold, you need to leave the desert."

"Oh darn," he replied. "I was afraid of that. I've always lived in the desert and don't really want to go anywhere else. I want to stay in the desert *and* find gold."

"Mister," said the girl, "if you stay here, you're never going to find gold."

The man protested, "But what if I try my hardest, and pray night and day, and use my very best sifting technique?"

The girl said, "You're fooling yourself if you expect to find gold in the desert. There will never be any gold here. Even if you try your hardest, pray night and day, and use your very best sifting technique, you won't succeed."

"But," replied the man, "as I told you before, I don't want to go anywhere else. I don't like to travel, and I'm very comfortable in the desert."

The girl said, "Sifting for gold in the desert is like trying to squeeze water out of a rock."

"You can't squeeze water out of a rock!" the man said.

The girl smiled playfully and handed him a small, hard, dry desert rock. "Go ahead and try," she said. "Squeeze it really hard." Just for fun, he gave the rock a squeeze. Of course, nothing came out of the rock.

She said, "Squeeze a little harder."

So the man squeezed with all his might, but no water came out.

The girl teased, "Maybe you're not doing it right. Maybe you need to twist it or sit on it or rub it—surely if you keep trying, you will squeeze some water out of that rock?"

The man replied, "No, I can't squeeze water out of this rock."

"And why is that?" the girl asked.

He stated, "Because there is no water in it."

"Exactly," said the girl, "and there is no gold in that sand. Go to where the gold is if you want to find the gold."

The man realized that the girl was very wise for her young years. He could stay where he was (and quit hoping to find gold) or move on to a new place where gold was plentiful (the word "plentiful" means LOTS of gold). Just *knowing* he had a choice made a difference.

THE BOTTOM LINE: GO for the gold!

9

Self-Control

Keep Your Lion on a Leash

Many things are better in moderation. Autonomy and leadership are to be respected, but cross the line into arrogance and a child will have few friends. Most of us admire confidence, but arguing with an oppositional 9-year-old is very tiresome.

The story that follows, *Keep Your Lion on a Leash,* is about learning self-control. It is designed for use with children who have problems with self-regulation or oppositional behavior. The strong-willed, somewhat oppositional child in this tale is determined to do things his way. His mother admires his individuality, yet that characteristic was likely more endearing to her when her son was a toddler than it is to her now. In families who do not set limits for their children, the children can become out-of-control non-compliant "brats."

It does not help to enter into power struggles with oppositional children. Drawing a line *in the sand* and daring them to cross it is likely to result in many crossed lines. Oppositional children need to be provided choices and opportunities to learn from their choices. Motivational interviewing and role-playing can be quite helpful.

The story is humorous, and the reader may experience admiration for "Sam" until he clearly crosses a line in wanting to do things his own way. Therapists will find this story helpful with families as they begin discussing rules and limit-setting. Children will smile as they recognize themselves and move less defensively into a discussion of their behavioral choices and styles of interaction.

KEEP YOUR LION ON A LEASH

Sam really liked to do things his own way. He just couldn't help it. His mother would say, "Please don't wipe your mouth on your shirt when you're eating." But Sam really *liked* wiping his mouth on his shirt. For one thing, the napkin took too much time. He also liked how all the food colors looked on his shirt—like a piece of art! So when his mother wasn't looking, he wiped his mouth on his shirt. Sometimes his mother caught him doing it and said, "Oh Sam, you always want to do things your own way." It was true—he was just that kind of boy.

By the way, did I tell you that Sam had a pet lion that lived in his bedroom? He got it for his birthday when it was just a baby. "That's it!" Sam had thought. "I'll call him Baby!"

The baby lion liked to run around Sam's room, and Sam taught him how to wrestle. What a fun pet to play with! It hid in Sam's closet and jumped out at him—"Peek-a-boo!" Baby purred real loud, too, like a motor running—he could feel it on his cheek when the lion cuddled up beside him to watch TV in his bedroom. Sam taught Baby tricks, like "stand up" and "beg for hot dogs." Baby listened to him better than the dog did!

As Sam grew, Baby grew, too. Soon, Baby was really *big* (his mouth was as big as Sam's head) and Sam's mother said, "Baby is so big now that you must keep him on a leash. He is a wild creature and doesn't know his own strength. He will hurt you or someone else without meaning to."

"Oh Mom," said Sam, rolling his eyes. "Baby is my friend, and he loves me. He would never hurt me."

"Trust me, Sam," answered his mother. "Baby is a lion, and it is his nature to hunt and attack. I want you to buy a leash today. If you let him off the leash, you won't be able to control him."

Sam didn't want to admit it (and would not admit it to his mother), but he was a little afraid of Baby now. Baby was bigger than Sam, and his teeth and claws were sharp and pointed. When Baby *roared*, he scared everyone in the house. So Sam decided to listen to his mother and bought a bright red collar and a nice strong leash.

From that day on, Sam kept Baby on the leash. He still made him do tricks, like fetch the dog (just kidding!!), and Baby still lay next to him and purred when they watched TV together in Sam's room.

But a part of Sam still wanted to do it his way—after all, Baby was his friend. He kind of let himself forget what his mother had said. He thought, "What Mom doesn't know won't hurt her. I'll try letting Baby off the leash for a few minutes. I trust Baby—I don't think he would ever hurt me!"

Sam looked Baby in the eye and quickly unhooked the leash from the lion's collar when his mother wasn't looking. "Good lion," said Sam.

But Baby opened his mouth and *roared* with a loud mean rumble. Sam backed away and said, "*Stay, Baby!*" Baby moved forward slowly, one step at a time, a wild look in his eye. The hair on the back of his neck stood up, his tail went up in the air, and his eyes narrowed. He looked like a wild lion! Baby swiped at Sam with a huge clawed paw and squatted down like he was ready to pounce.

Sam mumbled, "Oops, bad decision . . ." He saw how dangerous and wild Baby was off the leash. Sam did not know what to do, because any minute now he was going to get eaten alive! Then Sam had a sudden "aha." He ran out of his room and slammed the door behind him. "*Roar*," went Baby, as he clawed at the door. It was a very thick door, so for the moment, Sam was safe.

Sam dashed into the kitchen and grabbed 10 hot dogs out of the fridge. Baby *loved* hot dogs! But as Sam headed back down the hall toward his room, he saw his mother at his bedroom door, her hand on the doorknob. "What is all the noise in there?" Sam heard his mother say as she turned the doorknob.

"Oh *no*!" thought Sam. "Mom is going to get eaten alive!" He shouted, *"Mom, don't open the door!"*

But it was too late! The door started to open. "*Roar!*" Baby's head pushed out through the crack—so close that Sam's mother could feel his hot breath on her hand. She saw Baby's head just in time and managed to get the door closed before the lion could take a bite out of her. Her face was quite red and she did not look very happy.

Sam's mother backed away from the door and said sternly, her hands on her hips, "Sam, what have you done? That lion is off his leash!"

Sam did not answer her. He quickly opened his bedroom door a crack and threw the 10 hot dogs far into the room, behind Baby. When the lion turned around to eat them, Sam jumped into the room and quickly re-hooked the leash to Baby's collar.

Then Sam commanded, "*Baby, Stay!*" as he tugged on the leash, and Baby lay down with his head on his paws. He looked a little sad, as if to say, "Sam, I didn't want to hurt you or your mother. It is just my nature."

Sam ran over to where his mother was standing. "Mom, let me explain," he begged.

His mother shook her head "No" and held out her hand like a stop sign. "Oh boy," thought Sam, "I'm in real trouble, now."

His mother said, "Give me a minute, Sam. My heart is pounding and I need to calm down." Her face was still quite red.

In a few minutes, his mother had calmed back down. She said, "Sam, I know you like to do things your way, but doing things your way this time almost got us killed."

Sam replied, "Mom, I will leave Baby on his leash from now on."

His mother wanted to say, "I told you so," but she bit her lip (which means she did not say it). It was better to have Sam learn the lesson himself. Sam added, "I still like to do things my way, but I'll try to think first before I do something stupid."

His mother tried to hide a smile as she thought, "That's my Sam. He always likes to have his way. And wanting to have your way is not such a bad thing. My Sam is a boy with a real backbone and lots of courage."

Sam and Baby, of course, sat down to watch TV in Sam's bedroom. Sam held the leash firmly in his hand, and Baby purred to his heart's content.

THE BOTTOM LINE: Keep your lion on a leash!

10

Letting Go of Worries

The Burden Bag

The focus of *The Burden Bag* is worry reduction and letting go of burdens. Many children and teens *collect* negative experiences and carry them around in life, weighed down. The suggestion within this story is to let burdens go to lighten the load and not go "fishing" for them afterward.

The rabbit in this story is burdened by many worries; and children and families with whom I read this story have used it in different ways. One animated 8-year-old girl grabbed a rabbit puppet and acted out the story as it was read. When we got to the part of the story about throwing away burdens, she jumped up and began the action of tossing her burdens away with a big smile on her face. It was a turning point in her therapy, as she made up her mind that day to really *work at* not worrying so much.

A family that had been challenged by much adversity engaged in a family ritual after hearing the story. They used "magic" dissolvable rice paper to write down their personal burdens, then dissolved them in water (there is a brand-name paper called Dissolvo available at various sites on the internet).

The story requires little further introduction. It can be combined with play therapies or art activities focused on letting go of burdens. Families may wish to make paper-bag backpacks in which to place their burdens; and children love the idea of letting go of worry *for good*.

THE BURDEN BAG

Jack was a young rabbit that moved as slow as a turtle. Jack was not sick or old or physically challenged—he just moved very slowly. His forehead was lined, his eyes drooped, and even when he smiled, Jack Rabbit looked tired and sad.

One sunny day, Jack and a group of his friends were hopping through the meadow. The other rabbits were hopping with lots of energy. "Hippety, hippety hop" they went, but Jack was going "thud-drag . . . thud-drag . . ." at a very slow pace.

As the group hopped along, they came across a kindly older rabbit, a good friend of Jack's family. The older friend watched the hippety hopping and hop-thudding and scratched his head with his large rear foot.

"Jack Rabbit," he said, "you don't run or jump like the other young rabbits. You are moving slower than a turtle in mud!"

The older rabbit then saw that Jack was wearing a large, overstuffed, very heavy backpack. It pulled on Jack's shoulders, sagging halfway down to the ground! There was a label in big red letters on the outside of the backpack, but it wasn't Jack's name. It said *Jack's Burdens!* Burdens, by the way, are problems that worry you and weigh you down.

Jack's friend said, "Why are you carrying that heavy backpack? You could hop faster if you took it off."

Jack said firmly, "*No—I never* take it off."

His older friend asked, "Don't you take it off to eat?"

"No," Jack said, "not to eat."

"What about to sleep?"

"No," he said, "not to sleep."

"Well surely you take it off to play?"

By this time Jack felt a little impatient and said, "I *told* you I *never* take it off. Not even to play!"

The older rabbit was very curious. He knew it was really none of his business, but he still asked, "What's in it? Is it schoolbooks? Or rocks? It looks so heavy!"

Jack did not mind telling him what was in the backpack and said, "This is my bag of burdens. They *are* heavy!"

The older rabbit was still quite curious and asked, "Can I look inside it? I can't believe a young rabbit like you could have so many burdens."

Jack replied, ""You can look inside if you want." So the wise old rabbit went behind Jack, opened the backpack, and peered down inside. There were many Ziploc bags of burdens in the backpack. Each bag was neatly labeled with colored permanent marker.

The first bag, with a blue label, said, *Stupid Mistakes*. The second bag, with the green label, said *Rejections*. (Rejection is when someone you like stops liking you back.) A third bag of burdens said *Family Problems*.

The older rabbit took a peek inside the *Family Problems* bag and remarked, "Many of these family problems have other people's names on them. Why would you carry around someone else's problems?"

"I like to help out," said Jack.

The fourth bag of burdens smelled really *awful*, and it was labeled in purple: *Imperfections*. The young rabbit explained, "Those are things about me that aren't perfect, like my warts, my big feet, and my crooked teeth."

The wise rabbit said, "No one's perfect. If you want to jump like other rabbits, you need to get rid of these burdens. A rabbit is not meant to move as slow as a turtle!"

Jack argued with him and cried and pouted. He begged, "I've been collecting these burdens my whole life. Can't I just keep a few? I won't know what to do without them!"

"No," said the older rabbit, "it's time to let them go. You can carry around a few 'daily concerns,' if you like, but not burdens."

Finally, Jack agreed that the backpack was *very* heavy and kept him from enjoying his life. He knew he needed to lighten his load.

His friend said, "Come with me. I know just the place to take your burdens. It's a very special place, through the woods."

"Lead the way," said Jack.

Together they hopped down a rocky path and through the woods.

"Here it is," said Jack's friend, as they stopped before a beautiful lake. "This is a bottomless lake."

Jack said in disbelief, "*NO* bottom?"

"That's right," said his friend as he pointed toward the lake. "Look at the sign over there."

Jack looked where his friend pointed and saw a big sign next to the lake. It read, *NO FISHING ALLOWED*. His friend said, "If you throw something in there it is gone for good."

"Aha," said Jack. "I know what you want me to do. You want me to throw my burdens in that lake." He took a small step back, not sure he was quite ready to do what he needed to do.

"It's OK," said his friend. "You know what you need to do." Jack realized he was ready and nodded his head in agreement.

Jack took the backpack off, and his friend helped him take all the burden bags out. Together they unzipped all the bags. "OK, here we go!" said his friend, as he handed Jack a burden. Jack pulled his arm back as far as he could, took a deep breath, and then threw the burden with all his might. The burden flew out over the water and came down with a big "Plop!" Jack watched as it hit the water and sank below the surface.

Letting go of that first burden gave Jack courage. He threw the burdens out in the middle of the lake, one by one, and watched them sink.

As each burden hit the lake, Jack saw big circles of ripples spreading out on top of the water. As Jack watched the ripples spread out, his heart grew lighter and lighter. Before Jack knew it, he was standing on the edge of the lake with an empty backpack.

Jack had a sudden moment of doubt. "Oh my goodness, what have I done? What will I do with an empty backpack?"

His friend said, "Throw it in too."

Somewhat reluctantly, Jack threw his backpack into the lake and watched it sink. He suddenly felt hopeful and took a quick hop forward.

Jack thanked his friend for helping him and hopped home, his head held high. When he got home, he told his mother about his day, with great excitement.

"I'm proud of you, Jack," said his mother, "for having the courage to throw away your burden collection."

"Mom," said Jack, "I'm a little worried that sooner or later I'll be tempted to collect burdens again." Jack knew that collecting burdens was a bad habit. Everyone knows that it is hard to break a bad habit!

His mother suggested, "What you need is a new backpack!" She went to the rabbit hole closet and came back with a brand new backpack with thick cushioned straps. On the front pocket, it said, *Blessings*.

"What are *blessings*?" asked Jack.

"*Blessings*," replied his mother, "are good things, like carrots and lettuce and making new friends. When you notice a blessing during the day, stuff it in this bag. At the end of the day, you can count your blessings."

"I like that idea," said Jack. "But," he added, "what can I do if I have a bad day and start collecting burdens again?"

His mother answered, "If you start to collect burdens again, the lake is always a good backup plan. After all, you're only rabbit."

In case you did not know it, that's rabbit for "You're only human." It's what you say to someone when you want to remind him or her that no one is perfect and everyone makes mistakes. So whether you are "only rabbit" or "only human," you may want to do something to lighten your load. And don't forget to count your blessings!

THE BOTTOM LINE: Lighten your load and count your blessings!

11

Denial and Avoidance

The Hidey Hole

The Hidey Hole is simple and to the point, its message being *it is a good thing to pay attention to and face what is going on and not ignore dangers or take excessive risks.*

There are many reasons why children and their parents avoid talking about things or pretend that there are not problems: Sometimes a child judges that what is on his or her mind is *too bad* to talk about (abuse, eating disorder, domestic violence, substance abuse, the possibility of divorce, a secret adoption, a serious illness, and so on). Children may keep secrets within the family and have been told "not to tell." A parent may avoid the truth, fearing a child's reaction. Children and their parents avoid talking about things that create conflict or lead to painful feelings.

This story is ideal for early phases of treatment in which families or individuals *deny* having problems that are known to the therapist. They may be issues in the past that are unresolved or important family issues that are not yet discussed.

And yet the proverbial elephant in the living room must be discussed, sooner rather than later. It is a little like trying to work your way into cold water for a swim. You know that the water will feel warmer once you are in, but it can be hard to get past the initial colder temperature. Some swimmers plunge right in but others never get past putting in the big toe. This story helps a family or child *get used to the water* and provides a structure for sharing their stories. Once the reader takes the plunge, it is much easier to discuss the things he or she has been avoiding.

THE HIDEY HOLE

Ozzie Ostrich loved to walk and play outside, like most other ostriches his age. He really loved going across the street, climbing the small hill up to the train tracks, and then standing on the tracks. He could see for miles ahead and miles back when he stood right in the middle of the tracks on top of that small hill. He felt like king of the hill!

Now, of course, Ozzie's mother had told him over and over, "*Never* stand on the railroad tracks. They are dangerous and you could get hurt." He did not mean to disobey his mother, but it was a hard decision to make—whether to obey his mother or whether to feel like king of the hill on the railroad tracks.

Ozzie knew that trains were dangerous, but he always jumped off the tracks before the train got too close. As he stood on the tracks, he could hear the train whistle.

First, far off in the distance. "Whoo-whoo!" The whistle got louder and louder as the train got closer. *"Whoo-whoo!"* Ozzie felt the tracks rumbling through his tennis shoes, and the train got even closer. "*WHOO-WHOO*!" He knew it was time to jump when he saw the wheels turning.

One day Ozzie was walking along the tracks and saw a deep hole right in the middle of the tracks. He thought, "You know, I think my head would fit inside that hole!" So Ozzie stuck his head down inside the hole—it was a good fit. It was dark, quiet, and peaceful.

"Wow," he thought, "I like it inside the hole. It's quiet, and I can forget about my problems."

Ozzie started going to the tracks every day. Sometimes, he played king of the hill on the tracks; and when he had a bad day, he stuck his head inside the hole for some peace and quiet.

A couple of days later, Ozzie had a really bad day. He had an argument with his best friend Fred, and he got a bad grade on the spelling test. After school, Ozzie wanted to get away from it all. He ran over to the train tracks as fast as he could.

Ozzie ran up onto the tracks and stood in front of his favorite hole. Before he stuck his head in the hole, the young ostrich looked down the tracks to check for trains. Unfortunately, a train was coming. It was still far off in the distance, perhaps a couple of miles away, and it seemed to be moving slowly. Ozzie could faintly hear the whistle blowing. "Whoo-whoo!"

He thought, "I still have time to put my head in the hole, just for a minute."

So Ozzie put his head in the hole. It was dark, quiet, and cozy. He breathed a sigh of relief. He couldn't hear the train whistle from inside the hole, so Ozzie decided to pretend that the train wasn't coming.

Ozzie thought, "Can't see the train—the train's not coming! Can't hear the train—the train's not coming!" He said this over and over again. He said it so much that he started to believe it!

And when the tracks began to rumble and the train began to approach, Ozzie did not get off the tracks.

His friend Fred had come over to "make up" after the argument at school and saw Ozzie standing on the tracks. Fred saw the train getting closer and closer. Fred hollered, "Ozzie! Get off the tracks!" Of course Ozzie's head was inside the hole and he did not hear Fred hollering at him.

Fred knew he had to do something fast or Ozzie was going to get hit by the train. Fred dashed across the street and ran up to the tracks. He pulled Ozzie's head out of the hole and yanked him off the tracks right before the train zoomed past. Ozzie felt the wind blow his feathers and heard the train's "Whoo-whooooooooo!" as it whizzed by.

Ozzie and Fred were red in the face and panting. Their hearts were pounding! Ozzie realized he had nearly been killed. He said, "Whew! That was a close call! I'm never going to do *that* again."

"Exactly what were you doing?" asked Fred.

Ozzie replied, "I couldn't see or hear the train, so I pretended it wasn't coming."

His friend Fred exclaimed, "That was the stupidest thing I've ever seen! You're just lucky I happened to come by!" Fred added, "You need to keep your head aboveground and your eyes wide open to see what's coming!"

Ozzie thanked his friend over and over, and the two of them went to play in the park

Later that day, Ozzie had a "guilt attack" and told his mother what he had done and what had happened. His mother grounded him to the house for a week. "I want to be able to trust you and know you're safe," she said.

"I know, Mom," said Ozzie. "I'll keep my head aboveground from now on!"

THE BOTTOM LINE: What you don't see can hurt you!

II

SPECIFIC TREATMENT ISSUES

The stories in this section are tied to DSM-IV diagnoses or specific treatment issues and are targeted toward symptoms or problems of child and adolescent clients. Most of the metaphors may be used with other problems as well; for example, even though *The Twin in the Mirror* is targeted at children with eating disorders, the metaphor of confronting parts of oneself may be used with any child who needs to *talk back to* his or her negative thoughts and perceptions.

Depending on the child's age, the stories may be used in group, family, or individual cognitive behavioral treatment in conjunction with play modalities such as games, puppet play, or art/expressive therapies. The stories may be paraphrased for younger children and the good storyteller will stop often as he or she reads to engage the child and ask questions.

Therapists are encouraged to be creative and individualize techniques. Generally, the therapist should *utilize* the client's response in developing an intervention. Therapists are recommended to involve parents in all interventions so that they have a clear understanding of the child's perceptions and problems. Parents need to be able to *take the treatment home* and provide opportunities for the child to practice and gain competence in the home environment.

12

Performance Anxiety

The Grounded Eagle

The first story in this section, *The Grounded Eagle*, is written for anxious, worrying children with low self-efficacy. Such children avoid doing things for fear of negative outcomes. They may have specific phobias or generalized anxiety that impede performance or lead to avoidance of life situations. Their anxiety can interfere with performance in sports, classroom presentations, or the performing arts. The story suggests that visualization, practice, and exposure can help a child conquer his or her fears.

Children love hearing about Joe's dilemma and identify with his concerns. They chuckle at the young eagle trying to purchase tennis shoes (to avoid flying to Tennessee) yet understand his avoidance. Since it is extreme behavior for an eagle to fly to Tennessee from Kentucky, a child hearing Joe's story thinks, "I'm not that bad. I may avoid going to new places but I would never walk to Tennessee!" It is important to ask the child how he or she relates to Joe.

The story provides insight into how children think about danger, and how non-helpful it is for adults to deny danger or promise that nothing bad will ever happen. The metaphor of being "born to fly" is a great springboard for talking to a child about his or her strengths and coping skills. Joe becomes a friend and role model as the child works on his or her anxieties; and as the child celebrates with Joe at his success, that child begins to envision the possibility of his or her own success. Cognitive behavioral therapies such as relaxation, guided imagery, and in vivo exposure will parallel the story's themes. It is important to include parents in treatment and to *send the treatment home* to allow ongoing practice and reinforcement.

THE GROUNDED EAGLE

You might wonder why a young, handsome eagle named Joe had just walked into a department store in Louisville, Kentucky, and asked the stork-keeper to show him some size 8 tennis shoes. The stork-keeper certainly wondered the same thing. In case you did not know it, a stork-keeper is a stork (type of bird) that sells things in a department store. Joe the eagle had a lovely white head and beautiful long wings filled with shiny dark feathers. He had a nice, confident "strut," and his feathers rippled as he walked.

"Excuse me," said the stork-keeper to the eagle. "I hope you don't mind my asking—but what is a nice, young eagle like you doing shopping for tennis shoes? Everyone knows that eagles don't need tennis shoes."

"Well," answered Joe, "I'm getting ready to walk to Tennessee, and I need some really good tennis shoes to protect my feet."

The stork-keeper said to Joe, "You're going to *walk* to Tennessee? That makes no sense at all! Everyone knows that eagles fly." He added, "I know it's none of my business, but is there something wrong with your wings?"

Joe looked a little sheepish (that means he was slightly embarrassed). He stared down at the floor and replied, "No, my wings are fine. It's just that there are all sorts of things that could be dangerous for a flying eagle. I decided to walk to Tennessee. It will take a little bit longer, but at least I'll be safe."

The stork-keeper was surprised, because he didn't know that an eagle could be afraid of flying. After all, flying is an eagle's nature—his beautiful, strong wings can carry him very long distances. An eagle is born to fly! The stork-keeper asked, "So what kinds of things are you afraid of?"

Joe had a list of worries all ready to share with the stork-keeper. "I could fly into a tree in the fog or collide with an airplane. I could get struck by lightning or get caught in a thunderstorm. A hunter could shoot me or a tornado might blow me away. I could catch a cold up in the clouds and get pneumonia. A bigger eagle might attack me. I might fly in the wrong direction, get lost, and end up in Pennsylvania instead of Tennessee!"

He opened his beak to continue, but the stork-keeper stopped him and said, "You're right. There are many dangers up in the sky."

The young eagle was surprised. Grown-ups usually tried to tell him everything would be OK or that he would be perfectly safe. They sort of lied to him, to try to make him feel better. It didn't really help, because he knew that there were dangers up in the skies. It also didn't help that the daily news (in the paper and on the TV) talked about so many bad things.

The stork-keeper continued, "But worrying *too much* can keep you from living your life."

The young eagle protested, "The world is dangerous, especially up in the sky!"

The stork-keeper replied, "There are dangers on the ground as well as in the sky—there are wild animals in the woods and humans driving cars on the roads. You can't avoid all danger."

Joe protested again. "All I can think about lately is getting sick or hurt while flying."

The stork-keeper replied, "No one wants to get sick or hurt. Yet eagles are born to fly. You need to get back in the sky as soon as possible. If you sit around worrying about all the things that could go wrong, you'll never get back in sky."

The stork-keeper then asked, "Are there any good things about flying?"

Joe thought for a minute and replied, "There are some good things about flying. When I use my wings and soar, I feel free and strong. When I fly high in the sky, I can see for miles ahead. When I'm in the sky, I can see storms coming and take cover before they hit."

"Exactly!" said the stork-keeper. "Those are all good things about flying!"

Joe thought about what the stork-keeper had said. He knew he was born to fly. He didn't like walking, and it hurt his feet. It took too long to get places, and he couldn't see ahead to where he was going. He also was having trouble finding tennis shoes that fit an eagle's feet—for some reason, his claws kept getting in the way.

Joe thanked the stork-keeper for his help said, "OK, I've changed my mind. I'm not going to buy tennis shoes. I'm going to be brave and fly to Tennessee." He asked the stork-keeper, "Would you come cheer me on later today as I get back in the sky?" Joe wanted some encouragement. He knew there was a chance he would "eagle out" (that's eagle for "chicken out") right before he took off.

"Sure, Joe," said the stork-keeper. "I get off work at 4 PM. I'd be happy to watch you take off."

"Good," said Joe. "Then I really think I can do it. I'll meet you at 4 PM right behind the store. Thanks!"

So at 4 PM, the stork-keeper and Joe met behind the store. "Take a minute to relax," suggested the stork-keeper. "Close your eyes and pretend you are doing a perfect takeoff." So Joe closed his eyes and imagined himself doing just that. In his imagination, he could see his big wings spreading and could feel the wind lifting him up into the blue sky. He could see it so clearly, every step of his success.

Then he opened his eyes, looked at the stork-keeper, and took a deep breath. The stork-keeper gave him a "thumbs up" (with his big claw, of course, since he didn't have a thumb) as Joe leaped into the air and spread his beautiful wings. His wings were made to fly—they caught the air and lifted him up. Joe looked both ways as he took off, so he didn't fly into anyone or anything. As Joe flew higher and higher, he felt strong and free. Joe was meant to fly, and Tennessee was just a short flight away.

THE BOTTOM LINE: Let yourself soar like an eagle.

13

Parental Mental Illness

Call It Like It Is?

I once worked with a child in a group home. Her mother's odd behavior and inability to see things the way others saw them was a source of constant embarrassment to the little girl.

"Please turn my mom into a mom," she said. In this case, her mother had a dissociative disorder and had great difficulty keeping track of her life and her children. She tended to "reweave" the facts in most situations, and she had her own unique way of interpreting what went on in her family. It was not possible to "fix" the problems in the girl's mother (what she wanted us to do); but it was possible to help her love her mother as she was and to realize that the unusual behavior was not the girl's fault nor her responsibility to "fix."

There are a number of parent mental illnesses that are correlated with risk in child development: substance abuse or dependence, personality disorders, dissociative disorders, major depressive disorders, bipolar disorders, and psychotic disorders. Being raised in a family with a mentally ill parent can be quite stressful. Children in these families need to find resources and community supports in order to become resilient and grow up healthy.

Psycho-education is helpful with children in these families; and the story that follows, *Call It Like It Is?* represents the types of reality distortions children may face when presented with their parent's worldviews. Unless told otherwise, children will blame themselves for parental symptoms and are likely to be confused by the inconsistencies in the home. Children need to know it is OK to seek support outside the family and to have a safety plan (should be part of the parent recovery plan as well) for emergencies. The story is a good springboard to help the child discuss ways in which his or her parent is different and how he or she feels about that.

CALL IT LIKE IT IS?

Eleanor Elephant handed her son Elvis a big container of cookies and nudged him out the front door. "Have a great day, Elvis," she trumpeted, her trunk swinging wildly.

"OK, Mom," Elvis mumbled. It had been a bad week. On Monday, his mother had taken him to school, and on the way she landed in a sinkhole with him on her back. He flew 20 feet and had a bad headache all day from the rough landing.

"Just a *bump* in the road," she trumpeted loudly. "Climb back on, Elvis."

It was just like his mother to call a sinkhole a bump in the road . . .

"That's OK, Mom," replied Elvis. "I'll just walk to school. You can go on home."

On Wednesday, his mother had told him to find some clean socks to wear, because it was cold out. He couldn't find any. They were all in the washing machine from the night before. He knew that because he had done the wash.

He tried to sneak out the door without his mother seeing him, but she caught him and grabbed him roughly with her large trunk. She yelled at him for not wearing socks. "I told you to find your clean socks. You are a disobedient, disrespectful boy! Tonight you go to bed early!"

It was just like his mother to blame him for something that was her responsibility.

Finally it was Friday. His class was having a party that day, and his mother had decided at midnight the night before to make cookies for the party. The noise of clanging pans and the oven timer ringing had kept Elvis up, and his mother's singing while she baked did not help one bit.

At least, you might think, Elvis would be happy that his mother had baked cookies. But he was not. You will be grossed out when I tell you why.

Well, Elvis had awakened from a sound sleep when his mother started using the electric mixer to add the ingredients. He rubbed sleep out of his eyes and trudged into the kitchen.

"Hi, Elvis," called out his mom cheerily. "Guess what I'm doing?" Before he could answer, she said, "Baking cookies for your class!" Her trunk was swinging around wildly.

"Mom, it's midnight," said Elvis, looking at the clock. "Why are you baking cookies at midnight?"

"I couldn't sleep," said his mom. "So I thought, 'Why not?'"

Then his mom turned back to the mixer and scooped up a big measuring cup of brownish stuff. She dumped it in the bowl with the flour, vanilla, and baking soda.

"What's that stuff, Mom?" Elvis asked.

"It's *sugar*!" said his mom in a loud voice. "Can't you see?"

"Mom," said Elvis, "it doesn't look or smell like *sugar*."

"Sure it does," said his mom. "And it's in this container labeled *sugar*, right where I keep it."

Elvis, unfortunately, knew that they had run out of real *sugar* the week before. His mother had promised to buy some more, but she had forgotten.

Elvis had a *really bad* suspicion about what might be in the *sugar* container.

"Mom," Elvis asked, "where did you put the rest of the manure for the compost?"

In case you did not know it, compost is something you use on gardens to help them grow. Among other things, it has elephant manure in it. Manure is poop.

"I don't quite remember, Elvis," shouted his mother. "So *quit bothering me* and *go back to bed*." His mother was swinging her trunk more wildly than before and her tail was whipping back and forth.

Elvis knew it was a hopeless cause and went back to bed. He didn't sleep very well, though, and the next day, he took a plate of cookies with him with some misgiving. That means he was a little worried about what was *in* the cookies.

Once Elvis got halfway to school and he was out of sight of his mother, Elvis sniffed at the cookies. *Phew!* It was elephant manure, no question about it. Elvis gagged. His mother had confused elephant poop with *sugar* and the whole batch of cookies was baked with the nasty stuff.

It was just like his mother to call manure *sugar*.

Elvis walked into school crying in frustration and asked his teacher to speak with him privately for a minute. He told his teacher Ms. Snuggli what had happened and cried, "My mom is crazy! Why can't we make her see it like it is? Why can't she be normal like other parents? It's not fair!"

Ms. Snuggli hugged Elvis and said, "Elvis, I'm so sorry. Your mom has a mental illness. She can't help it, and we can't change her. You can love her the way she is and let us help you get through the things that happen."

Elvis replied, "Well, we can't eat these cookies. I know my mom is going to ask me how we liked them, and I'll have to lie to her."

Ms. Snuggli suggested, "Elvis, you can tell your mother that I appreciated her going to the trouble to make the cookies at midnight and that they were some of the most beautiful cookies I have seen. Don't say anything about whether we ate them. If she asks, tell her they were great cookies. After all, it's the thought that counts."

She added, "Sometimes you will have to avoid telling the whole truth, because your mom sees things differently. You can't change how she sees things but you have control over how you respond to her. Put a smile on your face when you can, give her a hug when you need a hug, and go to your room when you need some private time. I'm sure your neighbors the Monkeys would always welcome your company, and anytime you need to, you can talk to the school counselor."

Together, Elvis and Ms. Snuggli threw out the cookies. Elvis enjoyed the class party, and when he got home that day he told his mom that Ms. Snuggli thanked her for the time she took to bake the beautiful cookies. His mom was so pleased at the compliment that she never bothered to ask how they had tasted. Elvis gave his mom a big hug and went to his room to watch TV.

Elvis heard his mom singing loudly as she scrubbed the kitchen floor with a pair of his underwear, having confused it with her mop head. He actually smiled to himself. He thought, "My mom sure does and says a lot of weird things. But my teacher's right. Mom sees things differently. At least I know she doesn't do it on purpose or to embarrass me. She has a mental illness, and it isn't my fault or her fault."

Elvis was glad that he had talked to his teacher. He knew he could talk to the school counselor, who was a good listener, if he had a bad day.

Knowing and admitting that his mother had a mental illness gave Elvis courage. He found himself better able to cope with things at home, one day at a time. You might *not* be surprised to learn that Elvis offered to help the next time his mother decided to bake a batch of chocolate chip cookies. Of course, you have probably already figured out that Elvis added the sugar to the batter after his mother whipped up the eggs and butter—better to be safe than sorry!

THE BOTTOM LINE: Get through what you can't change!

14

Fitting in Socially (PDD/Asperger's Disorder)

The Bulldozer in the China Shop

Certain children and adolescents have deficient social skills and do not see themselves as others see them. They may be impulsive or socially awkward, intrusive or painfully shy. Some carry diagnoses within the DSM-IV disruptive behavior disorders or pervasive developmental disorders (PDD) categories. Those with Asperger's disorder are one group with significant social deficits.

Children and teens with Asperger's disorder or PDD NOS have poor reciprocal communication, may show undue interest in one specific area to the exclusion of others, have trouble transitioning from one activity to another, and do not understand their impact on others. They tend to "lecture" others rather than engage in two-way conversation; and their poor fine motor skills may lead to poor handwriting. Their clumsy gait and poor coordination may interfere with playing sports or riding a bicycle. Sensory sensitivity may result in these children wearing odd clothing combinations (they find certain textures irritating) and they are likely to button every button on a shirt in their obsessive need for completion.

Asperger's disorder presents new challenges during adolescence, as these teens are often "late bloomers" and subject to ridicule or rejection. Eventually they notice how different they are from other teens and may become depressed as they struggle to fit in. Sexual development (awareness and interest) is delayed as well (it parallels the delayed social development) although puberty is not, which leads to frustration.

The Bulldozer in the China Shop is about this type of individual with Asperger's disorder. The child may or may not recognize himself or herself in the story, but the child's parents surely will. The light, humorous presentation will allow them to talk more easily about the differences they observe in their child. The story conveys that change is possible through effort and skill development.

THE BULLDOZER IN THE CHINA SHOP

Byron Bulldozer was happy—a rare moment in Byron's history. He was happy because he had just gotten a new handheld game for his birthday. Usually, he was in a bad mood from falling down the stairs, wrecking his bike, or getting a paper back from a teacher marked in a red "D" for poor handwriting. Poor Byron was a real klutz, you know, the kind of kid that falls out of his seat all the time and trips over his untied shoelaces. He wore mismatched shirts and pants, stripes with checks and contrasting shades of blue. He buttoned his Polo shirts all the way up to the top—he said he "had to" although no one could figure out why.

Byron was a bit of a *slob*, too. When he ate, his food spilled all over his shirt and pants. He wiped his mouth on his sleeve and forgot to use a napkin. He usually sat alone at lunch. He talked too much about fossils and Star Wars, when other kids were trying to talk about homecoming or the next basketball game. And instead of looking people in the eye, Byron always looked away or down at his feet. Most kids thought he was pretty weird.

"Byron," his friend Bill often said as Byron talked on about something without taking a breath, "please remember that this is a conversation and not a lecture!"

"Oh, yeah," Byron would say. And then he would keep on talking. He didn't really care too much that his behavior seemed weird to other people. He liked being alone and enjoyed playing with handheld or video games. He *loved* the Discovery Channel and shows like Animal Planet or *Mythbusters*.

Byron was bigger than many kids his age. He was a bulldozer; and most of his classmates were backhoes. Byron stood out in the middle of all the backhoes. Unfortunately, Byron got into lots of trouble because of his size and poor coordination. The weekend before, Byron had gone to a china shop to buy something for his mom for Christmas. It is not a good idea for a bulldozer to go to a china shop, as you might imagine. Before he left the store, he had caused $200 worth of damage. People still talked about the time Byron went to the greenhouse to get some plants for his mother's garden. He forgot his blade was down and bulldozed a whole field of flowers.

Even though Byron was a loner, he wanted to belong and had one or two nerdy friends like himself. Byron had a secret crush on a girl but that's as far as it went. Most of his classmates had already been out on dates. He hadn't even kissed a girl yet. He didn't know if he *wanted* to kiss a girl, because it seemed like it would carry too many germs, but he wished there was a girl that *wanted* to kiss him.

Byron went to the school counselor and said, "What can I do to fit in better? The handwriting is clearly on the wall. If I keep doing the things I do, I'm never going to fit in. And I doubt there will ever be a girl that *wants* to kiss a guy like me."

His counselor knew a lot about bulldozers and the problems they have. He really wanted to help Byron. He answered, "Byron, it is possible that you can change some things to fit in better. If you want to try, it will take a lot of time and hard work."

"That's OK," said Byron. "I think I'm ready to do what I need to do to fit in better."

"Well," said the counselor, "I wonder if anyone has ever told you that you are a Transformer."

"What?!" shouted Byron loudly.

"Indoor voice, please," said the counselor. "You are a Transformer. But we thought we should wait to tell you until you were a bit older so that you would understand the instructions. Real change requires a certain level of maturity."

"I play with Transformers," said Byron. "But I didn't know that I *was* a Transformer. Exactly what can I transform into?"

"You can transform into a large cat," said the counselor. "But the transformation takes many steps and it will be hard to remember."

"What good is a cat?" Byron asked bluntly.

"Well," said the counselor, "a cat is sure footed and coordinated; it lands on its feet when it falls, and it is very observant. A cat likes to cuddle up but only when it wants to—it likes its independence. It can use its claws to protect itself but it can purr to communicate its pleasure. Cats are attractive and cat people tend to like them. All in all, they fit in better than a bulldozer and they are safe in china shops and greenhouses."

Byron asked the counselor for the instructions so that he could practice transformation. He met with the counselor every other week and practiced secretly, because he was embarrassed about making a change. Byron hated change.

It was a pretty funny process at times. His friend Bill helped him read and figure out the instructions. Byron missed a step the first time he tried to transform, and he turned himself into a fish with cat whiskers. The next time, he ended up with porcupine quills. Once he transformed himself into a giraffe that meowed!

After two years, on his 251st try, Byron realized that he finally looked and acted like a cat. The transformation had worked! Byron went to school and interacted as a cat that day. His friend Bill sat with him at lunch, and a girl he liked let him cuddle up next to her on a cafeteria bench. He purred loudly and was amazed when she petted him gently and kissed him on the head.

Byron was on cloud nine! Not only did girls like and talk to him now, but he had much better hygiene. Everyone knows that cats go to great effort to keep their coats clean and shiny. Byron thought he was probably meant to be a cat—he loved fish and chicken, and playing with the laser pointer in the science lab was great fun. Transforming back into a bulldozer would certainly be possible if the situation ever called for it, but for now Byron thought he might as well change his name to "Tom" (cat) and enjoy his new identity.

THE BOTTOM LINE: Transformation takes time!

15

Bedtime Anxiety

Things That Go Boo in the Night

This story, *Things That Go Boo in the Night,* utilizes the phenomenon of children's magical thinking to provide suggestions for dealing with nighttime fears. Many children have fears about sleeping alone in their beds, and unwittingly, their parents allow them to come into their bed for comfort. Children may be 8, 10, and 12 years old and still want to sleep with their parents. Once in a while, that is not a problem, but as a rule, children need to learn to self-soothe and manage their anxiety about sleeping alone.

Once children are in the parent's bed, it can be difficult to get them back into their own beds. This story is appealing to children, as the main character conquers her fears and provides an efficacious role model for fearful children. The story acknowledges that adults are not always sympathetic to children's fears yet it is clear that the goal is to overcome those fears.

Parents and children reading this story will be able to utilize many of the girl's solutions, and a therapist can help the family with exposure and anxiety reduction techniques.

THINGS THAT GO BOO IN THE NIGHT

The little girl was afraid to go to bed at night. You see, night after night, monsters came into her bedroom. Her mother kept saying, "Don't be silly—there's no such thing as monsters. Monsters are just make-believe."

But at night, the girl's bedroom became a dark, scary place, and make-believe monsters somehow got into her room.

"Perhaps," she thought, "they come in through that small crack between my window and the windowsill."

The girl was not surprised that her mother did not believe her. After all, only *children* could see the make-believe monsters. Some looked like ghosts. Others looked like monsters the girl had seen in a cartoon movie.

The monsters liked to scare children, and they ate "fear" for their midnight snack! So guess what they did when they got hungry during the night? Yes, you guessed it! They came into a child's bedroom to stir up a little fear and then quickly gobbled it down.

The little girl did not want to sleep in her own bed—not with monsters in her room! "Please can I sleep with you tonight? Can I have one more hug and kiss?" she would ask. She avoided going to sleep with, "I want a drink of water" or "I have to go to the bathroom." Her mother usually told her to go back to bed—she just didn't understand.

One night the girl woke up because she really did have to go to the bathroom. As she started to get out of bed she heard a voice coming from her closet.

"Yoo-hoo, little girl! Yoo-hoo!"

"Am I dreaming?" the girl wondered. But no, she was wide awake.

She heard the voice again. "Yoo-hoo, little girl!"

And even though the closet door was closed, it looked like someone had turned on the closet light. She could see a crack of light at the bottom of the door.

The girl was a little scared, but the voice sounded friendly, so she went to the closet door and peeked in.

"Oh my goodness!" she exclaimed.

"*Shhh!*" said the friendly creature sitting before her on the closet floor. "Your parents might hear you." The creature was smiling, which is why the girl thought it looked friendly. It was dressed in rainbow colors, had long cotton candy hair, and was glowing in the dark.

"Hello," said the creature. "I'm your monster manager, ready for service!"

The girl asked, "What is a monster manager?"

The creature replied, "I do monster removal for children."

"Why haven't I ever seen you before?" asked the girl.

The monster manager said, "I'm usually invisible. I work in children's bedrooms after they are asleep. I check closets and under the beds. I teach children how to be brave and chase monsters away."

"Oh," sighed the girl, "I really need your help."

The monster manager had a clipboard and took notes as the girl talked about her fears of make-believe monsters. The manager said, "I can help you with this problem, and you need a good night's sleep."

"Do you know about the *Monsters Hate* rules?" asked the manager.

The girl replied, "I've never heard of the *Monsters Hate* rules."

"It's very simple," said the manager. "They are things that monsters hate."

So the manager pulled a piece of white paper out of her pocket, put on a pair of gold-rimmed glasses, and with the glasses perched on her nose, she squinted her eyes and began to read:

Rule Number One: *Monsters Hate Monster Spray*

Rule Number Two: *Monsters Hate Bright Light*

Rule Number Three: *Monsters Hate Brave Kids*

Rule Number Four: *Monsters Hate the Monster Manager*

Rule Number Five: *Monsters Hate the Smell of Parents*

The monster manager said to the girl, "If you follow the *Monsters Hate* rules, the monsters will quit coming to your room and go bother someone else!"

She continued, "Let's start with Rule Number One: *Monsters Hate Monster Spray*."

"Where do I find monster spray?" asked the girl.

The monster manager put a finger to its mouth and said, "*Shhh*," as it led the girl by the hand into the kitchen and pointed to a can on a shelf. "There is your monster spray." It was just a can of air freshener!

The girl asked, "How can air freshener make monsters disappear?"

The manager replied, "At night it turns into monster spray. Monsters hate the smell, and they disappear when they are sprayed. Monsters hate the smell so much that they won't come into a room that has been sprayed."

The girl said, "Let me ask Mom if I can use it." So the little girl called to her mother, who was watching TV. "Mom, my room has a funny smell in it. Can I use the air freshener?"

Her mom said, "You're supposed to be in bed," but added, "OK, take the can, spray your room, and then please go back to bed. You need your sleep."

The girl went back to her room and sprayed the *monster spray* in the air, in her closet, under her bed, and at the window. She put the can of *monster spray* on her bed by her pillow, just in case she needed it during the night.

"There," she said. "Now I'm ready for those monsters!"

"Good job," said her manager.

Next, Rule Number Two: *Monsters Hate Bright Light*. The manager said, "You need to ask your mother for some light."

"I know!" said the girl. "I can ask my mother for a nightlight. And I have a flashlight in my desk drawer for if the electricity goes out."

So the little girl ran into the other room again. "Mom, can I have a nightlight? I'm scared of the dark. If I have some light I'll sleep better."

Her mother said, "I thought you went back to bed." But the mother loved her daughter, so she gave her a small nightlight and a big hug. "Now please go back to bed."

The girl went back to her bedroom. With the nightlight on, the room was dark enough to sleep in but light enough to let the girl see things more clearly.

Then the girl asked the monster manager, "What should I do when I wake up in the middle of the night and feel really scared? When I'm scared, my heart pounds and I can hardly breathe."

The monster manager replied, "There is a special way to breathe when you're scared. Breathe in slowly, like sucking through a straw. You breathe in courage, and courage makes your tummy rise. Then puff your breath out really slowly, like blowing up a balloon. When you breathe out like this, you blow out all the fear."

The girl tried this—"slurp, slurp, slurp" in went her breath, and "puff, puff, puff" out—no more fear!

The manager explained, "As you get braver, the monsters will leave and not come back. After all, they eat fear for their midnight snack. No fear? No monster food! They'll have to find their snack somewhere else."

Then the monster manager stepped back into the girl's closet. "I have to leave now, to go help someone else. But every night, I'll come back to make my rounds. I'll be invisible, of course."

"Your rounds?" asked the girl.

"When I make my rounds, I'll check your closet and under your bed, so you won't have to. Use your monster spray if you need to, and everything will be fine."

The girl saw a quick flash of bright light inside her closet, and the monster manager was gone.

The girl went to sleep more easily that night, because she knew she was safe, and she had good dreams. She kept her monster spray and her flashlight by her pillow, just in case.

And, by the way, monsters REALLY hate parents. So if a child gets REALLY scared and nothing else works, that child can ask mom or dad to come into the room for a quick hug. Just the smell of a parent in the room sends monsters running. That's for sure!

THE BOTTOM LINE: Use what you have to fight your fears.

16

Obsessive-Compulsive Symptoms

The Magic Stone

Children with obsessive-compulsive symptoms relate immediately to the main character in *The Magic Stone*. Their eyes grow wide as they realize that OCD Frog has a problem similar to their own that keeps him from enjoying life.

Most children with obsessive-compulsive disorder find their symptoms baffling. They feel *weird* and are delighted that the main character in this story, OCD Frog, shares their dilemma. And even children who are simply worriers will find the intervention, exposure with relaxation, helpful.

The story includes a good description of OCD symptoms from the frog's point of view, and children can distance themselves from their own fears as they chuckle at the frog's concerns. There is a helpful friend in the story that coaches, guides, and make suggestions but the frog himself makes the decision to change his behavior. It is clear that change is a process and that relapse is possible, but OCD Frog discovers that his quality of life will be better if he gives up his compulsive habits and rituals.

The story should be read with the child and parent, as it will be the parent who will help the child carry out practice (exposure and response prevention) at home.

THE MAGIC STONE

Oliver Cornelius Danbury Frog, better known by his friends as OCD, had a serious problem. He was better known as OCD because no one wanted to say a long name like Oliver Cornelius Danbury, and it took him way too long to write it! OCD Frog was so exhausted that he could not enjoy the swamp anymore. The word "exhausted," in case you did not know it, means that he was very tired all the time.

And why, you might ask, was OCD so exhausted? Well, first of all, OCD spent *a lot* of time worrying that something bad might happen. For example, he was worried that a big bird might eat his mother, and he spent a lot of time watching the sky for birds.

OCD also spent *a lot* of time every day hopping and croaking. His legs ached so much and his poor throat was sore, but he just couldn't stop. Oh, he knew that frogs were born to hop—but he *had* to hop 126 times every time he went out to hop, and he was getting very tired.

He also could not stop croaking. Yes, OCD knew that croaking was something all the frogs did at night in the swamp, but he *had* to croak 2,003 times in a very high voice. All the other frogs croaked in their deep "rivet" tones, and there he was croaking and croaking and croaking like a soprano. In case you did not know it, a soprano is a singer who sings in a very high voice. OCD just could not stop.

OCD Frog had a secret. He *knew* deep inside that if he did *not* hop 126 times his mother would die. He also *knew* that by croaking 2,003 times, he was keeping the whole frog world safe and was preventing some horrible disaster. He wasn't quite sure what type of disaster. He just *knew* he had to keep croaking. Other frogs did not believe these things, but it did not stop OCD himself from hopping and croaking.

OCD had another serious, secret problem that was quite embarrassing. He was deathly afraid that the flies he ate were too dirty—he believed that the germs would make him sick. So OCD snuck away when he was ready to eat and washed off each and every fly 10 times. He was losing weight—you can imagine how long it took to wash all those flies! Other frogs laughed at OCD for doing this, but it did not stop him from washing flies.

A wise old neighborhood owl had been watching this poor frog from his perch high in the trees above the swamp. He could see that OCD needed his help. He decided that a little "magic" was in order.

So he swooped down to talk to OCD Frog and said, "My name is Hoot Owl. You don't know *whooooo* I am, but I am here to help you. I understand what a serious mission you think you have in life. You want to keep your mother safe, and you really care about our swamp world. I know you don't want to get sick on dirty flies."

He continued, "Unfortunately, *you-whoooo* can't keep bad things from happening just by hopping, croaking, and washing flies. But you are afraid to stop doing these things just in case they are helping."

OCD Frog said, "Oh my goodness—that's it exactly!" He added, "You know, I feel absolutely *miserable*!" (In case you don't know it, "miserable" is when someone is very unhappy and frustrated, too.) "I am exhausted, and I don't have any fun anymore. I don't *want* to keep doing these things, but I can't stop myself. What can I do?"

The young frog realized he had forgotten his manners and added, "Pleased to meet you, Hoot Owl. My name is OCD Frog."

Hoot Owl nodded his head back at the introduction. "Give me a minute," he said. "I need to think about what you might do to take your mind off all your worries." As he thought and thought about what OCD could do, Hoot Owl turned his head almost all the way around and scratched the back of his neck with his sharp beak.

He turned his feathery head back around and said, "You just need something to focus on instead of your worries. You need a special magic stone. You'll find your magic stone over there by the stream. You might want to pick up that smooth brown one with the speckles on it or that pretty black and white one. Go pick one up, now, and then come back."

So OCD went over by the stream. "How do I know which one to pick?" he called back to Hoot Owl.

"It doesn't matter," said Hoot. "Whichever one appeals to you the most. The magic is inside you, after all. The stone just helps it work."

OCD picked up a particularly pretty smooth brown stone, and brought it back.

Hoot Owl said, "Now, touch the stone and say some magic words. You get to make up the magic words. Doing that will take your mind off your worries."

OCD Frog said, "What do I do after I say the magic words?"

Hoot Owl replied, "After you say the magic words, take a BIG breath in and out, to help the magic work. When you touch the stone and say these magic words, you will be able to hop, croak, and eat flies normally, like all the other frogs. You can touch the stone and everything will be OK. Try it and see."

The frog said, "How shall I touch it? Should I touch it 56 times? Should I use my tongue or my foot? Should I use both? Should I count while I touch and do the touches in just the right order?"

The owl smiled kindly and replied, "No, touch it only once. If you touch it more than once the magic won't work. You can touch it with your tongue *or* foot. Not both. No counting! When you feel the urge to hop 126 times, touch the stone once and say the magic words. Then check on your mother. When you feel the urge to croak 2,003 times, touch the stone once instead and say the magic words. Then go check on the frogs in the swamp. You can say the words out loud or inside your head. When you get the urge to wash flies, say the magic words. Then eat the flies."

Hoot Owl added, "Now I'm not saying this will be easy for you. It's no big deal if you mess up once in a while. Just keep trying. If you relax and focus on other things instead of your worries, things will get better a little at a time."

So OCD Frog picked up the stone Hoot Owl had pointed out, took it home, and kept it close to him at all times. About a week later, OCD saw a bird. He began to think that the bird would eat his mother and got very anxious! He almost started hopping 126 times, but instead, he remembered what the owl had said. With hope, he touched the stone once, said the magic words, and took a *big* breath. His heart was pounding and he could hardly breathe! Soon he calmed down a little and went to check on his mother. She was fine! That night, he got the urge to wash a few flies, but the stone's magic helped, and he ate the flies just as they were, fresh and delicious! Sure enough, he did not get sick.

OCD Frog did better from that day on. He continued to use his magic stone, and little by little he gained control over his worries. He knew deep inside that it was not the stone that helped him but his resolve to stop doing the things he had been doing; in any case, it was nice to have something to hold on to when he started to worry. Once in a while, he worried, "What if this happened?" or "What if that happened?" But those times, and his anxiety, passed. OCD had more time to do the things he needed to do. He thanked Hoot Owl for his help. With all the time he saved, he had more time to play with the other frogs in the swamp. And you might be interested in knowing that OCD's mother lived a long and happy life!

THE BOTTOM LINE: A little worry goes a long way.

17

Eating Disorders

The Twin in the Mirror

The Twin in the Mirror is a story about a girl with an eating disorder who learns to talk back to her negative self-perception, depicted as her twin in the mirror. Client ambivalence (health vs. self-destruction) often resembles a familiar cartoon scenario. The cartoon character has a devil on one shoulder and an angel on the other, both arguing persuasively in the character's head. The angel argues in favor of what is in the person's best interest. The devil tries to convince the character to do the "bad" thing and ignore the angel. In the cartoon, the angel usually wins.

Not so true in real life. The client's self-destructive urges often win, at the expense of that person's very being. Eating disorders are one area where self-destructive beliefs and perceptions may "win out." Anorexia nervosa is too often lethal and bulimia has serious health ramifications.

To argue with one's own destructive side is quite self-efficacious. The girl in this story is coached to refute the irrational beliefs that are present in eating-disordered individuals. Children and adolescents who experience an inner battle will find the CBT technique in this story empowering.

THE TWIN IN THE MIRROR

Once upon a time a girl and her parents lived together in the *House of Rules.* There were many rules to follow, about how to eat, what to say, and how to behave. The rules of the house were posted in every room of the house. Each rule started with the words, "You should . . ." or "You should not . . ." The rules taught everyone how to "Should Upon" themselves. The girl's parents had also been raised in the *House of Rules,* so they taught their daughter to follow the rules without questioning.

The girl was smart and talented. She tried hard to be good and to please her parents. She hoped that someday, if she followed all the rules, she might become *perfect.*

One rule was, "If someone asks, 'How are you?' say, 'I'm just fine' even if you aren't." Another rule was, "If you can't say something nice, don't say anything at all." A third rule was, "Don't worry—act happy." So the girl and her parents said only "nice" things to one another and lived "happily" in their "just fine" *House of Rules.*

There was just one problem. The girl had many worries she kept to herself while she pretended to be "just fine." She worried about her grades, because she wanted to have straight As but got a B+ in math. She worried that she didn't have enough friends. She worried she would get in trouble if she ever told her parents about her "not so nice" worries . . .

One morning, the girl stood in front of her bedroom mirror to check her hair before leaving for school. She suddenly heard a loud, shrill voice. "What are *you* looking at? You don't need to stare, you know!"

Where was that voice coming from? "Don't just stand there looking stupid!" continued the voice. "Don't look so surprised; I'm right in front of you!" The girl could hardly believe her eyes and ears—her identical twin was talking to her from within the mirror! The twin spoke again. "Cat got your tongue? No wonder you don't have many friends. You follow all those dumb rules, but you are ugly and fat!"

The twin was so rude! The girl did not like how the twin was talking and started to leave the room. The twin saw her leaving and shouted in a bossy voice, "You come back here and listen to me—I'm not finished!" The girl slowly walked back to the mirror and peered in at her twin. The twin said, "That's better. You know what you need to do to *really* be happy?"

Now that caught the girl's attention—she would love to *really* be happy. "No," said the girl. "What do I need to do to *really* be happy?"

The twin replied, "You need to lose weight. When you lose some weight, you won't look fat anymore, and then you will be happy. Take a look in the mirror and see for yourself."

The girl took a good look in the mirror and realized that her twin was right. Her body had started to change recently; in fact, there were soft curves in places that used to be lean and firm, probably because her parents always made her eat everything on her plate at dinner. She felt clumsy and awkward.

The girl looked back in the mirror and said to her twin, "OK, I believe you're telling me the truth. I'm too fat and need to lose weight. When I do that, then I will *really* be happy."

The girl's twin coached her daily to help her lose weight. She made her do 100 sit-ups and jog around the block 5 times. The girl skipped meals, which everyone knows is bad for your health. She weighed herself every day, sometimes twice a day, and she trusted her twin in the mirror to tell her the truth.

"You're still too fat," said the twin. The twin eyed her critically and demanded she lose more and more weight.

The girl did everything her twin ordered, but she still wasn't *really* happy. She got thinner and thinner. Her parents did not notice at first that she had gotten too thin. When the family doctor pointed it out, they tried to make the girl eat more at meals. They told her if she gained weight everything would be all right again.

Eventually her parents took her to see a wise helper. The helper asked the girl lots of questions. Then the helper said, "If you want to get better and be happy, you will have to stop listening to the twin in the mirror and find a way to talk back to her."

"Why would I want to do that?" asked the girl.

The helper replied, "Your twin lies to you. You are not fat, but she blinds you to how you really look."

The girl said, "That can't be true—she would never lie to me. She is my best friend."

The helper disagreed, "She does not act like much of a friend. A friend is on *your* side and sees the *best* in you."

The helper encouraged the girl to go home that day and talk back to the twin in the mirror. "Stick up for yourself. Don't let her boss you. If you keep listening to her, you will not get better."

There was a long silence as the girl thought about what the helper said. She had been losing weight for many months, and her twin still told her she was too fat.

She told the helper, "OK, I'll talk back to her. I don't believe she lies to me, but I guess I don't have to listen to everything she says."

Later that afternoon, at home, the girl was ready to face her twin. The girl went into her room, stood in front of the mirror, looked her twin in the eye, and said calmly but firmly, "You haven't been telling me the truth, and I don't think you have been acting like much of a friend!"

The twin replied, in a bossy tone of voice, "I'm the only friend you have!"

The girl declared, "Then I think I need some new friends—friends that will like me the way I am."

The twin looked mad when the girl said that—she pouted and refused to talk to the girl anymore that day.

Over the next few weeks, the girl continued to talk back to her twin. It got easier each time she did it. When the twin said, "You're too fat," she replied, "I am not too fat. In fact, I am probably too thin." When the twin said, "You will be *really* happy if you lose weight," the girl replied, "Losing weight won't make me *really* happy. I have lost a lot of weight, and I am still unhappy."

The girl was proud at standing up for herself, and she even said to the twin, "I'm not going to let you—or my weight—control my life anymore." You may be surprised to hear that when the twin dared her to weigh herself every day, she put away the scale. That made the twin really mad, and she pouted for a whole week!

The girl continued to meet with her helper, and during one of the talks, the helper said, "You're doing a great job talking back to your twin. Now it's time for you and your parents to have some new rules."

"New rules?" asked the girl. The girl did not think her parents wanted any new rules.

"Yes," said the helper. "The old ones weren't working. Let's try something new."

So the helper invited the girl and her parents to a meeting the very next week. As the meeting began, the helper said, "I know you love one another. I think you are ready for some new rules, so you can show your love in a new way. I'm going to read them to you, and then please tell me what you think."

1. No one is perfect
2. Strive to be ordinary
3. Do something fun each day
4. Celebrate small successes
5. Success is not about your weight
6. Nothing is too bad to talk about
7. Love yourself first
8. Change takes time
9. The only person you can change is yourself
10. Live one day at a time

The girl's mother said, "Of course no one is perfect. But what do these new rules have to do with our daughter getting better? The rules don't make sense. All she needs to do is eat and gain weight."

The helper said, "We all want your daughter to be healthy. She does need to eat and gain some weight. But to get better, she needs to do more than eat and gain weight. Your daughter needs to love herself and learn to live her own life. And she needs you to love her and help her do that."

Hearing the helper say that gave the girl confidence to speak up to her parents. She said in a firm voice, "I think the helper is right. I need to love myself. And I need you to love me as I am."

"You know we love you," said her parents.

The girl replied, "You love who you think I am. I'm not even sure who I am yet, but I'm going to find out."

She continued, "I'd like to try the new rules at home—what do we have to lose?"

The girl had realized that getting healthy was not about eating or food—it was about loving herself and being free to grow up. With or without her parents' support, that is what she needed to do.

The girl's parents weren't sure about the new rules, but when they heard what their daughter and the helper said, they decided to give the new rules a try. So the girl and her parents went home and began to use the new rules. It was not easy. They sometimes went back to the old rules, but as they practiced the new rules, they got better at it, one day at a time.

It was a little like learning to ride a two-wheeler bicycle. You know, you get on the bike and feel quite unsteady and wobbly. You fall now and then, but you pick yourself back up and try again. And while you're on that bike, your parents are running along beside you, one hand on the seat, cheering you on and letting go every once in a while until you finally get your balance. The girl's parents eventually learned to let go and the girl "got her balance." She reminded herself that one day at a time, she was finally getting better.

Then one day, her helper said, "You know, it's probably time to get rid of that old mirror. You might want to find a new mirror that reflects who you really are." The girl thought about it and agreed with the helper.

Before she could change her mind, the girl went home and took down the old mirror. "Here, Mom," she said. "We can donate this old mirror to the thrift store. I need a new mirror that reflects who I really am."

While they were at the thrift store, the girl found just the thing. It was sitting in a dusty corner of the store, as if it was waiting for her. It was a pretty mirror with soft, built-in lights. She bought it, took it home, and hung it up in her room. The soft light brightened up her room, and as she stood in front of it, she heard a voice, "Hello there! Thanks for bringing me home."

What??? As the girl looked in the mirror, there was that twin again. Or was it? This twin looked just like the other twin, but she was smiling, and her eyes were friendly and bright. Her voice was soft and kind. No, this was someone new.

The twin said with a smile, "No, I'm not her. I'm here to cheer you on, not criticize you. I'll tell you the truth, sometimes things that you don't want to hear. I'll let you see yourself as you really are."

The girl realized that this new twin would be a real friend and help her change her view of herself. After all, happiness comes from what we choose to pay attention to and how we interpret the things in our lives. Change takes time, so the girl and her parents kept talking to the helper. They followed the new rules, began seeing things in a new way, and allowed their love for one another to shatter the illusions they had lived with for so long.

THE BOTTOM LINE: See yourself as you REALLY are.

18

Depression

A Tough Nut to Crack

Depression results in changed self-perception, black-and-white thinking, negativity or irritability, filtering out positive events, and hopeless predictions. Depressed children become isolated and withdrawn, reducing their participation in formerly enjoyed activities. They have interpersonal difficulties as they become oversensitive to criticism or teasing and react in strongly negative ways toward peers.

The following story, *A Tough Nut to Crack,* is about a geode who hates his appearance and believes he is an ugly, dirty, rocky individual. Through the extraordinary efforts of a friend, the geode comes to understand that his beauty, which has been untapped and unrecognized, lies within. He opens up to those around him and finally shows them his inner aspects.

Using this story in conjunction with CBT play therapies and positive psychology techniques such as gratitude logs helps depressed children address and cope with the myriad of symptoms that occur in child depressive disorders. Pointing out the good that lies within helps depressed children broaden their focus and develop self-efficacy and positive self-esteem.

A TOUGH NUT TO CRACK

Gerry Geode was feeling sorry for himself as he sat on the side of a hill, in the middle of a big rock pile. It was a very large rocky hill, all dusty and gray. Gerry was the son of a giant gray boulder, a real *chip off the old block,* and the dusty hill was his home. You might want to know why Gerry was feeling sorry for himself, since rocks usually don't complain about much. A week before, Gerry had gone on a school field trip to the science museum in the city. At the science museum, some beautiful gemstones, rocks, and minerals had been on special exhibit—there were purple amethyst, white quartz, and black onyx. Gerry and his friends had ooh'd and ah'd as they saw the lovely exhibit.

Gerry had been pretty satisfied with his life before the field trip. He was a sort-of-ordinary type of rock: round, bumpy, and gray. He had rough spots all over him. He was medium size and medium weight, just like his friends. He had been rough, gray, and a little hardheaded his whole life; but so was everyone else in his world. Gerry now knew there was a world outside his own. He began to view himself and his life in a different light. He had feelings of shame and self-disgust for the very first time.

Gerry thought, "My life sucks. I'm not good enough. I don't like how I look. My home is ugly. I feel different, now!"

Gerry's mood, energy, and behavior had been affected by his new view of his world and of himself. He was *bored* all the time and he was too tired to do the things he used to do. He no longer wanted to roll down the hill with his friends. He envied the beautiful gemstones, rocks, and minerals he had seen at the museum. They had something special that he didn't have. No one ooh'd or ah'd over Gerry.

Gerry thought, "I wish I was something really special. I wish I had a special color or a special talent. At least my friend Lava can tell people that she once was part of a live volcano. I'm good for nothing!"

As you can tell, Gerry was depressed. The more depressed Gerry got, the grouchier he acted toward his friends; and when his parents asked him to do his homework or chores, Gerry rolled off into a dusty, gray corner and pretended he didn't hear them. He had trouble sleeping at night and thought more than once about rolling in front of an oncoming ATV, to end it all by smashing himself to pieces.

An older friend that lived on the hillside was concerned about Gerry and asked Gerry's parents if he could take him on an outing to the nearby river to cheer him up. They played in the sun and soaked in the river's waters all afternoon, until Gerry's friend decided to bring up his concerns.

"Gerry," said the friend, "you need to stop comparing yourself to the gemstones, rocks, and minerals at the museum. You are fine just the way you are."

"No, I'm not," said Gerry in an irritated voice. "I'm good for nothing. I'm ugly, gray, and ordinary."

"That's not true," said his friend. "Have you forgotten that some of our beauty comes from within?"

"What do you mean?" Gerry replied. "There is nothing inside me. I'm just a lumpy, bumpy rock! Everybody hates me!"

His friend reminded him, "You are a kind, faithful friend, and people used to enjoy being around you. But your attitude has changed, and no one wants to hang around you."

The friend added, "You're a geode. Maybe you need to open up and look inside. Everyone has good things inside. You need to find your beauty within. "

Gerry didn't believe his friend. But his friend had taken the time to invite Gerry on the outing to the river, so Gerry decided to humor him. That means Gerry decided to open up and prove his friend wrong.

Gerry bounced across the rocky ground by the river. Crack, *crack*, CRACK! Gerry cracked his outside shell open and then stared in amazement. He was speechless.

"See, Gerry," pointed out his friend. "You are a geode. Geodes are rocks with beautiful crystals inside just like the purple amethyst ones you saw at the museum. There is no easy way of telling what is inside a geode until it is cut open or broken apart. You can find geodes in places like Indiana, Iowa, Missouri, Kentucky, and Utah."

Can you guess why Gerry was speechless? Yes, gerry, plain and gray on the outside, was filled with beautiful purple amethyst crystals. As the sun caught them, the crystals sparked. You never would have guessed what was inside Gerry by looking at his rocky, rough exterior!

"I had no idea," said Gerry, "of what was inside me. I'm special after all."

"Gerry," reminded his friend. "We are all special. You just need to focus on what is inside and not judge yourself by your looks. After all, no one should judge a geode by its cover."

Gerry was a tough nut to crack. When he had a bad day, he sometimes forgot about his crystals. When he was in a bad mood, he felt like he was only a gray, bumpy rock. At those times, Gerry's friend reminded him, just as you and I sometimes need a good reminder, to pay attention to what was on the inside.

THE BOTTOM LINE: Be more than meets the eye!

19

Learning Difficulties

Swimming in Hurricanes

The puppy in *Swimming in Hurricanes* does not understand the concept of a *learning disability* and labels himself as *stupid*. When children have difficulty reading, spelling, writing, understanding language, or following directions, they compare themselves to others and fall short. They try hard to learn and struggle with slow processing speed or working memory deficits. This story is helpful in portraying learning disorders as forces outside the child's control (as opposed to something bad within the child), while encouraging the child to *keep his or her head above water* and *accept help*.

Teachers may view a child with learning disorders as *unmotivated* or even *lazy*. A teacher with this perception is less likely to offer extra help to a child. Parents may believe that the child could do the work *if he tried harder*, and this can result in long hours of homework and frustration.

When a child and parent have a better understanding of learning disorders, they can figure out how the child learns best and advocate for school accommodations that will maximize success.

SWIMMING IN HURRICANES

Rufus was failing puppy school, even though he tried hard to learn. He went to class every day with his owner, listened to the teacher, and tried his best to pay attention. The problem was that nothing stuck in his brain. "I'm so stupid," thought Rufus.

Other puppies' brains soaked things up like a sponge. Rufus often forgot what the teacher had said—things just went "in one ear and out the next!" The teacher would say, "Stay," and he would "come." At home, he forgot what he had been taught in school and could not figure out how to do his homework.

Sometimes during class he did not understand what the teacher was saying, but he was too embarrassed to ask questions. Other puppies made fun of him when the teacher wasn't looking and called him "Rufus Dufus." (In case you did not know it, "dufus" is a mean word for someone that is not very smart.) When other puppies teased him, Rufus put his tail between his legs and hid in the corner. "I'm so stupid!" he thought.

All in all, puppy school was a miserable, awful, boring place to be. His "stay" teacher said he was "unmotivated," "lazy," and did not "perform up to his potential." This made Rufus feel really bad. Sometimes Rufus would skip school and play with the stray dogs on garbage day.

His owner, his parents, and the "fetch" teacher told him he was really smart but had learning problems, but he didn't believe them. Rufus thought, "No, those grown-ups are wrong. What smart dog can't even learn to 'sit' or 'fetch'? I am just a stupid puppy."

Now Rufus could do many other things. He could play basket-bone, run really fast, and was a very good swimmer. In fact, Rufus was a better swimmer than most of the other puppies. He could jump in the river to fetch a ball and swim back to shore quicker than you could blink! "Big deal," he sighed. "What does swimming matter when I am failing puppy school?"

Two weeks later, the Olympics were on TV. In case you didn't know, the Olympics takes place over a very exciting week where the best athletes from all over the world compete for medals. Rufus and his father squatted down to watch the Olympic swimmer dogs swim the 100-meter doggy paddle. "Wow" barked Rufus as he watched the very best Olympic swimmer dog swim with all his might and make a new world record. "That's what I want to be someday," said Rufus. "I want to be an Olympic swimmer dog!"

Rufus's dad had a sudden thought. "Rufus," barked his father, "if an Olympic swimmer dog tried to swim in the middle of a hurricane, what would happen to him?"

Rufus thought that was a very silly question. He knew what would happen. He had seen pictures of a hurricane with its 100-mile-per-hour winds and huge flooding waves. "That Olympic swimmer dog would drown," said Rufus.

His father said, "Yes, he would drown." He paused and said, "So that must mean that he is a bad swimmer, a very stupid, incompetent swimmer."

Rufus thought about it and replied, "No, he's still a great swimmer, an Olympic swimmer dog."

His father then asked, "If he's such a good swimmer, why would he drown?"

Rufus said, "You know that no one can swim in the middle of a hurricane. Not even an Olympic swimmer dog!"

His father smiled and said, "You're right, Rufus. Even an Olympic swimmer dog will drown in the wind, rain, and high waves of a hurricane. That doesn't mean he's a bad swimmer. The storm prevents his success."

The puppy barked, "But what does that have to do with me?"

His father replied, "Sometimes even a smart dog has trouble learning, especially if he has 'hurricane size' learning problems."

Rufus began to catch on. He replied, "You're saying I'm not stupid at all—my learning problems just make it harder for me to remember things."

His dad agreed and added, "The learning problems are like the hurricane's wind and rain. If we can calm them down, it will be easier for you to learn. We want to help you and so do your teachers. Don't be afraid to ask for help."

Rufus went to sleep that night and dreamed that he was swimming in a hurricane. He had on a big life jacket that kept his head above water. He kicked hard to stay afloat, and soon a huge ship came and rescued him from the waves. He was wet and cold but he had survived.

The next day at puppy training school, Rufus decided that he would work hard and do his best. He practiced things over and over without getting bored or frustrated. He discovered he could pay better attention by barking to himself.

The next week, Rufus asked the teacher for help when he was confused about the difference between "fetch" and "stay," and he was surprised that he did much better on the "fetch" test later that week. Rufus's parents had helped him study for the test, and it helped him remember better. On his own, he had taken notes and looked at them before the test. All of these things really made a difference!

After two weeks, Rufus had learned how to "fetch," "sit," "stay," and "heel!" Now he knew that as he got help and worked hard, he would keep his head above water and "survive" life's storms.

THE BOTTOM LINE: Keep your head above water and avoid storms.

20

Divorce

Enough Love to Go Around

Research suggests that it is best for parents to stay together while raising children, except when they are exposing their children to highly stressful circumstances such as drug trafficking, domestic violence, constant fighting, or abuse.

The divorce process is stressful, even when parents work hard to keep their children out of the middle. There may be negative outcomes; for example teens may develop mistrust of committed relationships when they are caught off guard by their parents' divorce. Young children may regress emotionally or behaviorally, and school-age children may continue to hope that their parents will re-unite. Families going through divorce may have financial problems due to additional living expenses. And children often feel ambivalence toward those that their parents date or remarry.

The cat in this story feels torn as her parents go through divorce. She feels disloyal toward her mother in liking her father's new partner and does not understand that she has *enough love to go around.*

The story's metaphor of love opens up Kit Kat's mind to new possibilities in her family relationships.

ENOUGH LOVE TO GO AROUND

"Yeowwwl!" heard all the neighbors, who quickly closed their windows to block out the noise. Those Siamese cats that lived on the corner were fighting again! And boy, when Mr. and Mrs. Kat had an argument, there was hair-raising, spitting, and *loud* meowing. You may not know this, but Siamese cats have a very loud "yeowl!" You could hear their arguments all the way down the street. After an argument, Mr. Kat often took off down the street like a rocket, spitting with flash and fire.

This had gone on for as long as Kit Kat, their daughter, could remember. She wished her parents would stop fighting and try to get along. Kit Kat often went outside to chase mice and leaves, just to get away from the noise.

Kit Kat's favorite times were when Mommy and Daddy would "make up" after an argument, with sandpapery kisses. Then the whole cat family would curl up together in the picture window to watch birds. Sometimes they ate catnip to have a little fun—it made them so happy they ran around in circles! But the good times never lasted long, and sooner or later there was another fight.

One evening, when the family was sitting at the kitchen table after a nice fish dinner, Mr. and Mrs. Kat told their children they had some bad news to discuss. "Is someone sick?" asked Kit Kat.

"No," said her parents, "no one is sick."

"Did Daddy lose his job?" asked Kit Kat's sister.

"No," said Daddy, "I still have my job."

"Then what is it?" asked the children.

Mr. and Mrs. Kat said, "Daddy and I have grown apart and don't love each other anymore. We fight too much. It isn't good for our family to live like this, so we are going to get a divorce. Daddy Cat is going to move out and live somewhere else. We think this is best for all of us."

Kit Kat knew that some parents get divorced, but she never thought it would happen to *her* family. She said, "You have been fighting for years—why would you get a divorce now?"

"It's for the best," her parents said again.

Kit Kat hissed, "Well, I think it's the *worssst* thing that has ever happened," and she ran to her room to cry herself to sleep.

In the days ahead, Kit Kat did things to try to get her parents to stay together. She pouted and cried, stomped her feet, and told lies, but nothing worked. Her parents had made up their minds. Daddy had already moved to a new house, and Mommy seemed less grouchy. The house seemed VERY quiet.

Soon Kit Kat's parents (and their lawyers) went to court. The judge said the divorce was "final" and gave them a paper that said they weren't married anymore. The judge "ordered" that both of the parents would take care of the children. Kit Kat and her brothers and sisters would take turns staying with Mommy Kat and Daddy Kat. So that's what they did.

Kit Kat's parents did try to get along better after the divorce, "for the sake of the children." She still wished her family had stayed together. Kit daydreamed about the "good old days" of catnip and bird watching. She still hoped that someday her parents might get back together.

Time passed, and one day when Kit Kat went to Daddy Kat's house, she saw a stranger lady cat standing by her daddy at the front door. She wasn't a Siamese cat—she had a black coat of fur with white spots on her face and paws. Her daddy and the black and white cat were kind of cuddling and swishing their tails together.

"Who is *she*?" said Kit Kat to her daddy, in a sort of mean voice.

Her daddy ignored the mean voice and said, "This is my friend Alley Cat. We have decided to get married, and she will be your new step-mom cat. You will grow to love her as I do."

Kit Kat was very upset! She thought, "I liked things the way they were. If Daddy gets married again, then he will *never* get back together with Mommy Kat."

Kit Kat didn't want to share her daddy with Alley. And she secretly hated black and white cats. That night as her Daddy tucked her into bed she hissed at him, "You may love that black cat, Daddy, but I *never* will!"

Yet as Kit Kat spent time with Daddy and Alley, she could see that Daddy was happy. Daddy and Alley laughed a lot together, and they only used their claws to give back scratches when they had an itch.

And as Kit Kat got to know Alley better, she discovered she was a very nice cat. Alley had a nice purr and gave the children good fish to eat. She licked Kit Kat's fur to clean it off and made sure she got plenty of sleep. There were times that Kit Kat even forgot she had vowed to never love Alley.

And now, Kit Kat had a problem. "One plus one equals two," Kit Kat thought. "I only have two pieces of love—one for my mommy and one for my daddy. If one plus one equals two, then I don't have any love left for Alley." Kit Kat worried, "I can't take the piece of love that belongs to Mommy and give it to Alley. I just don't know what to do!"

Kit Kat continued to worry about how to split up her love until the Friday night that Daddy announced, "Pack your bags—we're going to the beach!" Kit Kat swished her tail with excitement and went to pack her small suitcase. She loved going to the beach. Each summer when they went to the beach, Kit Kat got to play *Chase the Seagulls*. She had never been able to catch one, since they flew away so fast, but it was good exercise and fun to try.

Kit Kat also loved watching the white-tipped ocean waves. The waves made a splendid "whoosh!" as they reached the shore. At the end of the day, Kit Kat and her family curled up on the sand to watch the sunset and then, under the night stars, they ate piles of yummy dead fish that had washed up on the beach.

So as soon as they were all packed, Daddy, Alley, and the rest of Kit Kat's family jumped into the back of a Sea and Shore Ocean Fish Delivery truck and headed off to the beach. As soon as they arrived, Kit Kat raced out to the beach. She stood in the shallow water of the ocean and watched the waves as they crashed in, one after another. The water seemed to go on forever, as far as Kit Kat could see.

Suddenly, Kit Kat had an "Aha!" moment. In case you do not know what an "aha" moment is, it is when you suddenly see something in a new way. Kit Kat thought, "Love is like the ocean. The water never runs out." She purred with delight and played *Chase the Seagulls* on the beach for the rest of the afternoon.

Later that night, Kit Kat ate lots of yummy dead fish for supper, and then she curled up on the beach to watch the sunset. It was a lovely sunset, with pink and orange colors spreading above the horizon! Soon, the lovely hues dimmed as the blue-black of night appeared. Kit Kat purred with contentment, tired from her busy day, and she marveled at the beauty of the night sky. Hundreds of winking stars had come out, and the star-filled sky seemed to go on forever, as far as the eye could see.

Kit Kat suddenly had another "Aha!" moment. "My goodness," she thought, "love is like the stars in the night sky. They fill the sky, and there are so many stars that you can't even count them. I have enough love to go around—enough for everyone!"

Kit Kat began to purr. Her worry was gone, and she arched her back as she gave a big stretch. She now knew that the love in her heart was like the powerful ocean waves and the twinkling stars in the sky—it would never run out.

THE BOTTOM LINE: There's always room for more (love)!

21

Panic Attacks

The Bee and the Butterfly

Anxiety disorders run in families, and children with anxious parents may develop generalized anxiety disorder, phobias, panic disorder, or agoraphobia. Children may also develop anxiety in response to life circumstances.

Flutter-by, the main character in *The Bee and the Butterfly*, has a phobia of dogs and birds. She experiences anticipatory anxiety and avoids life situations where she might encounter one of these animals. Eventually, she becomes isolated and withdraws from contact with her friends.

Children with high levels of anxiety will go to great lengths to avoid feared situations. Their parents may unwittingly *protect* them rather than help them face their fears.

In treating anxious children it is important to provide exposure to the feared situations, and parents must be included in the child's treatment. Guided imagery, systematic desensitization, successive approximation, and live exposure are all helpful interventions.

THE BEE AND THE BUTTERFLY (dedicated to Laura)

A butterfly named Flutter-by fluttered in a zigzag pattern through the flower garden. Her shiny wings, with such beautiful shades of color, shimmered in the sunlight. But Flutter-by was acting a little strange. She had just left the public library and was talking to herself as she flew across the garden. She lectured sternly, "Danger is everywhere. Don't talk to strangers. Nothing is safe!" Then Flutter-by flew away from the garden and into the nearby woods.

Flutter-by was looking for a safe place to hide. She exclaimed, "There it is—just the place!" and headed straight for the rocky edge of a stream. The rocks there made a little cave into which she flew. As she landed on a rock in the dark hiding place, she gave a deep sigh of relief. "Finally safe!" she whispered to herself.

A bird, a dog, and a book at the library had spoiled her carefree life as a butterfly.

First, the bird . . . That morning, a bird had pecked at her, and Flutter-by narrowly escaped with her life. It was a "close call."

Next, the dog . . . That afternoon, a dog had snapped at her. Flutter-by thought later that maybe he was trying to play, but he had big teeth, and he could have hurt her.

"What about the book?" you might ask, since most butterflies don't read. But Flutter-by liked to read, and after the dog snapped at her, she flew to the library to read, since libraries are quiet, safe places to calm down when you are upset.

At the library, Flutter-by found a book about butterflies. "Butterflies," the book said, "are the most helpless of insects. They are the victims of the insect world. Butterflies have no way to protect or defend themselves. Birds and dogs are common predators of butterflies." (In case you did not know it, a victim is someone that gets hurt or bullied, and a predator is something that can hurt, attack, or eat you.)

Some butterflies have "protective coloring," but not Flutter-by. Butterflies with protective coloring have marks on their wings that look like eyes, and the "eyes" scare off other animals that might eat them. Some butterflies taste so bad that other animals don't want to eat them, but not Flutter-by. The book convinced Flutter-by that the garden was a dangerous place. That is why she flew into the woods to find a safe place to hide.

From that day on, Flutter-by lived in her cave by the stream in the woods. She missed the flowers and sweet smells of the garden, but she wanted to be safe.

Flutter-by tried to enjoy her life in the woods, but she still worried about possible dangers. She never flew too far from her cave, *just in case*. Flutter-by would see movement in a tree and think, "Is that a bird over there?" Then she would look closer. No, it was just a moving leaf. A few minutes later she would see something dark and think, "Is that a dog behind that tree?" No, it was just a shadow. And if she flew anywhere near a bird, she wondered, "Is it a nice bird or a mean bird? If it's a mean bird, it might try to eat me!" One day she saw a flock of birds in the trees above her and got so nervous she could hardly breathe.

"Maybe I'm having a heart attack," she thought. Then she remembered that butterflies don't have heart attacks (or hearts) and sighed in relief.

About a week later, a small honey bee was buzzing around the opening to Flutter-by's cave. He called to her, "Flutter-by, where are you? Yoo-hoo! Yoo-hoo!"

"What do you want?" called out Flutter-by.

Honey Bee said, "I haven't seen you flying in the garden lately and got a little worried. Why are you inside that dark cave?" He added, "I miss playing with you in the flowers."

Flutter-by poked her head out of the cave and replied, "Hello, Bee. How nice of you to check on me! I miss you, too. I am trying to stay safe. After all, I am the most helpless of all insects and have no way to protect myself."

She added, "I wish I could be a honey bee like you. You have a built-in stinger to protect yourself."

Honey Bee laughed. Flutter-by was annoyed. "How dare you laugh?" she retorted. "This is very serious stuff!"

Honey Bee did not mean to upset her and explained, "I only laughed because sometimes I watch you and wish that I could be a butterfly."

Flutter-by said, "Really? You wish you were a butterfly? Are you crazy?"

Honey Bee replied, "Honey bees all look alike. I wish I didn't look just like every other bee. There are many types of butterflies, and they are all the colors of the rainbow."

He continued, "Everyone knows that bees have stingers, but we have to be very careful about our stingers."

"Why do you have to be careful about your stingers?" asked Flutter-by.

Honey Bee replied, "Once we sting someone or something, we die. It is not a very nice weapon if using it will kill you!"

"Oh my goodness," said Flutter-by. "I had no idea that honey bees die after using their stingers!"

Honey Bee added, "Bees live in large groups, and we have to work hard all day to gather pollen. We take orders from our queen, and our lives are very dull. I wish I had your freedom to fly around."

"And," continued Honey Bee, "no one really likes bees—dogs try to eat us, and humans try to stomp on us. No one wants to get stung, so no one comes too close. People love butterflies because of their delicate beauty."

Flutter-by knew her friend had made some good points, but she argued, "I *am* the most helpless species and have no way to protect myself."

The bee replied, "That's true. But butterflies have good vision and are good fliers. You can use your eyes to be on the lookout for danger; use your mind to outsmart it; and use your wings to fly quickly away from danger when it comes."

He added, "I'm on a work break right now. Won't you please come out of hiding and play with me in the garden?" Flutter-by thought about what Honey Bee had said. She really missed the garden.

She called out to Honey Bee, "Do you see any birds or dogs?"

"No," he said. "All clear!" So Flutter-by poked her antennae out, then her head, finally the rest of her. She flew out of the cave, through the dark woods, into the sunlight of the garden. What fun she had playing with Honey Bee in the lilac bushes, even though she kept looking for dogs and birds! After a week of flying from the cave to the garden to play with Honey Bee, Flutter-by decided that she would give the garden life another chance.

Later that day, Flutter-by saw a dog. She got really nervous and almost flew back to the cave. But she remembered what Honey Bee had said and fluttered quietly right above the dog's head. The dog hardly noticed she was there.

"I did it!" she cheered. "I faced my fear!" Flutter-by fluttered in pride, and the flowers, bees, and other butterflies all clapped in joy at her fine accomplishment!

THE BOTTOM LINE: Come out of hiding and face your fears.

22

Attention Deficit Symptoms

The Magic Glasses

Becky, the main character in *The Magic Glasses*, has trouble paying attention and keeping track of things for school. She finds it hard to meet school demands, and she uses avoidance and denial to keep the truth from her parents.

Children with ADD cope in different ways with school demands. Some lie about having homework; others forget to turn it in. Some pretend their grades are OK until report cards come out; others procrastinate until the last minute, then try to catch up. It is not uncommon for ADD children to be labeled *unmotivated* or *lazy* by their teachers and parents.

Female ADD is under-diagnosed and anxiety may co-occur. This story focuses on the ways in which girls with ADD cope with the demands for school achievement and how their frustration can lead to avoidance and denial of problems.

The story may be used in conjunction with CBT interventions for improving attention, concentration, self-monitoring, self-control and self-reinforcement. Parents need to be involved in the treatment in order to coordinate efforts between school and home.

THE MAGIC GLASSES

Becky hadn't done her spelling homework—even after her dad reminded her right after supper. She was supposed to write out 10 spelling words and study them for a test the next day. Instead, she watched her favorite TV show and played with her dollhouse. The next thing she knew, her dad was saying, "Becky, it is 8 o'clock and time for bed!"

When people asked Becky how she liked school, she usually replied, "I like PE, library, music, art, lunch, and recess." Becky didn't like the classes where she had to listen carefully, take notes, or do homework. She had trouble paying attention and being organized.

In case you don't know it, "organized" means knowing where you put things and remembering what you are supposed to do. Becky often forgot where she put things and what she was supposed to do. She sometimes did her homework but it would get lost in her messy backpack, so she didn't turn it in.

Becky often forgot things. One afternoon, Becky told her father she would do her math homework right after her favorite cartoon. Instead, after her favorite cartoon, Becky painted her fingernails in a very pretty pink. Another day, when her mother asked her to go to her room to pick up her clothes, Becky said, "OK, Mom" and went to her room. When her mother went to check on her, she was playing dress-up, with clothes all over the floor. "I'm sorry, Mom," she said. "I forgot what I came in here to do."

After school one day, Becky walked across the street to play with her friend Heather. As Becky walked to Heather's house, she kicked at the grass. Something shiny in the grass by the curb caught her eye. Becky looked closer—it was a pair of sunglasses catching the sunlight. They were very pretty, and the lenses were dark, with lovely shades of purple. Becky picked up the glasses and tried them on. WOW! Everything looked different.

A bossy loud voice startled her. "Little girl! Little girl!" Becky jumped in surprise. The voice continued, "Little girl, I'm right on your very nose!"

My goodness! It was the glasses—they were talking! Becky started to take them off, but the glasses said, "No, Becky, please don't take me off!"

Becky said, "I must be imaging things, because glasses can't talk!"

The glasses said, "I am magic glasses. When you wear me, you'll feel good and you can ignore your problems at school!"

Becky said, "Wait till I tell my mom about YOU!"

The glasses whispered back, "If you tell anyone about me, the magic will be gone."

So Becky decided to keep the magic a secret. When she got home that day, her mother, who was cooking dinner, said, "Where did you get those glasses?"

Becky replied, "Oh, I found them in the grass. Aren't they pretty?" Her mother agreed they were pretty and went back to cooking dinner.

From that day on, Becky wore the glasses all the time. At school, the glasses whispered to her during class, and she paid even less attention to the teacher. She didn't study for the weekly spelling tests or do her homework. When she started to do her homework, the glasses would whisper, "Come on, Becky—let's play dress-up. You don't want to do your boring homework." It was true—Becky always got bored after about 5 minutes of doing homework.

Becky's grades had dropped from Bs to Cs. The glasses whispered, "It's OK, Becky. You don't really care that much about school." That was true, too. All Becky really cared about was PE, library, music, art, lunch, and recess.

The glasses said, "Becky, don't tell your parents the truth. If you tell them the truth they'll be upset. Just tell your parents you don't have any homework; or tell them you already did it and it's in your backpack. Tell them you did great on the spelling test. What they don't know won't hurt them."

Becky did not want to lie to her parents, but she lied anyway. She didn't want to get in trouble or disappoint her parents. And guess what? Her parents believed her lies. When her parents asked, "How is school?" Becky replied, "School is going fine, I'm getting all As and Bs."

Her mother gave her a hug and said, "I'm really proud of you!"

"Good girl," whispered the glasses to Becky. "What they don't know won't hurt them."

When her father asked, "Do you have any homework tonight?" Becky replied, "Dad, I did it as soon as I got home and put it in my backpack."

Her father gave Becky a hug and said, "I'm really proud of you!"

"Good girl," whispered the glasses to Becky. "What they don't know won't hurt them."

When her mother asked, "How did you do on the spelling test yesterday?" Becky said, "I only missed 1 word." She had really missed 5 words, but her mother said, "Good job. That calls for a treat!"

Her parents gave her a bowl of ice cream for doing her homework without being told and getting a good grade on the spelling test. Becky felt bad for lying to them, but she really liked ice cream.

Becky's teacher *was* concerned about her. Becky had never been a very organized student and had trouble paying attention, but it had gotten much worse. The teacher decided to send a note home to Becky's parents. "Becky," she said as she handed her the note, "please give this note to your parents."

"Oh-oh," Becky said on the way home. "Now I'm in trouble. My parents will really get mad that I'm not doing my work."

The glasses whispered to Becky, "What they don't know won't hurt them. Just throw the note away."

So Becky hid the note in her backpack where her mother wouldn't find it and later threw it away. Then Becky and the glasses went to Becky's room to play dress-up and dollhouse.

The next day, Becky told her teacher, "I gave my parents the note and promised them I would do better from now on."

Soon, Becky was failing spelling and math. "I know you can do better," said her teacher. "You just need to pay attention and do your work." The teacher tried hard to get Becky's attention—she put Becky's seat close to hers and often called out her name. But Becky still didn't do her work. Most of the time, Becky daydreamed while she drew colorful pictures on her papers.

The teacher decided to call Becky's parents, to let them know that Becky was doing worse, not better. That night, after Becky had already gone to bed, she heard the phone ring. She heard her parents say, "How nice to hear from you! We are so pleased with Becky's progress, lately!"

There was a long pause. "Oh-oh," whispered the glasses. "I think the teacher is going to spill the beans!" In case you do not know it, spilling the beans means someone is going to tell the truth. In this case it means the teacher was going to tell Becky's parents the truth about Becky's problems at school.

Becky couldn't hear what was being said but her mother sounded upset. Becky's heart began to beat very fast and she felt a little sick to her stomach. She heard her mother hang up the phone. She heard her father ask her mother what was wrong, and then she just heard hushed voices. Both of her parents sounded very upset. Every once in a while she heard a few words like "why," "how," "lie," and "homework."

Becky asked the glasses, "Do you have any smart ideas, now?"

The glasses replied, "No, I don't. I think that the jig is up." In case you do not know it, the "jig is up" means you have been caught at whatever you were doing and you are probably in trouble. Becky knew "the jig was up" before her parents even came into her room.

Yes, that is the next thing that happened. Both of Becky's parents came into her room. She tried to pretend she was asleep, but her mother said, "Becky, wake up. We really need to talk with you."

Becky opened her eyes. Her mother looked very sad. Her father was frowning and had wrinkles on his forehead. Becky's mother said, "Your teacher said that you are failing math and spelling. She said you haven't turned in any homework for a long time. We can't understand why you lied to us. Why didn't you tell us the truth?"

Becky started to cry and said, "I'm so sorry I lied. Even when I tried my hardest, I couldn't pay attention at school. I hate doing homework. I like to play and have fun. So when I found the magic glasses . . ."

The glasses interrupted Becky to whisper, "No, Becky, don't tell them about me! Remember, if you tell anyone about me, the magic will be gone forever!"

Her mother asked, "*Magic* glasses?"

"NO, BECKY, NO!" cried the glasses.

Becky ignored the glasses. "Mom, remember the glasses I found outside. Well, they are really magic glasses."

As Becky told her parents about the magic, suddenly, "POOF!" A wisp of pink smoke came out of the glasses, and Becky knew the magic was gone.

She continued, "The magic glasses helped me avoid my problems. Lying to you and my teacher just seemed like the best thing to do. The glasses told me, 'What they don't know won't hurt them.'"

Becky's parents said sadly, "That's not true. Lying to us did hurt us. When we don't know the truth we can't help you."

"I know that now," said Becky. "Lying to you did hurt you. And it hurt me, too. My grades are worse, and now no one will trust me. I need to pay attention in school and do my homework."

"Here, Mom," said Becky as she handed the glasses to her mother. "You can donate these to the thrift store, and some little girl can use them to play dress-up."

Becky's parents told her she was grounded for a week. The next morning, Becky found it hard to open her eyes. One eye at a time, she looked around. Everything in her room looked normal. Her mother was standing there with a caring look on her face. She gave Becky a big hug and said, "Welcome back to the real world!"

The magic was gone. Becky went back to school that day and only missed 3 words on the spelling test. The magic was gone. Becky found a new friend who also hated math and asked to sit with her at lunch. The magic was gone. Becky started to take some medication and went to counseling to help her pay attention. The magic was gone. When Becky had a bad day, she colored a picture or listened to her favorite music. The magic was gone. One day at a time, with her eyes wide open, Becky was learning to accept herself and live in the real world.

THE BOTTOM LINE: Pay attention to what matters.

Appendix A

Take-It-Home Questions and Activities

CHAPTER 1: ATTENTION SEEKING

Children

Draw a picture of Henry the Peacock as you imagine him. Hint—you can trace your hand to draw a peacock and then color it the way you like.

- Do I want to be like Henry? Why or why not?
- How am I like Henry?
- How am I like the other animals?
- When do I have trouble sharing?
- When do I want the most attention from others?
- Who do I "bug" the most for attention?
- How am I special?
- Everyone has things to be proud of—what do I like best about myself?

Adolescents and Adults

- What about me am I proud of? What are my special talents?
- How do I seek attention from others?
- Do I ever "overdo it" or compete for attention?
- How do I feel when I'm around a "Henry" who demands attention from everyone else?
- How do I turn people off? How does this make me feel?
- Am I more of a giver or more of a taker when I am with others?
- Is it hard for me to "strut" my stuff?
- When am I jealous of others?

- If we do anything to excess it can become annoying to others. What do I think I do to excess that might bother others?

CHAPTER 2: BULLYING AND ANGER MANAGEMENT

Children

Draw a picture of the dragon being a mean bully and another picture of the dragon being nice. Discuss how the dragon is different when he is being helpful.

- How am I like the dragon?
- Who do I pick on or bully?
- Have others ever bullied me? How does that make me feel?
- Have I ever watched a bully hurt someone else? How did that make me feel and what did I do?
- How do I act like the dragon toward others (my parents, teacher, brother or sister, friends, etc.)?
- How did the dragon feel when he was acting bossy?
- How did the dragon feel when others were afraid of him?
- What else could the dragon do or say to convince people that he has changed?

Adolescents and Adults

- How does my behavior offend others?
- When do I treat others badly?
- What types of people "trigger" me, i.e. "push my buttons"?
- When have I felt bullied or pushed around?
- What makes it hard for me to stick up for myself?
- In what ways have I tried to control others? What motivated me to do that? Did it work?
- "Low self-esteem can lead to bossy or controlling behavior." Do I think this is true? How might that happen?

CHAPTER 3: UNCONDITIONAL POSITIVE SELF-REGARD

Children

Use strips of paper to weave a tapestry placemat. Pick out colors you don't like and write things about you that you don't like on those pieces of paper. Pick out colors you do like and write things you like about yourself on those pieces of paper. Weave them into a placemat. Then take out the pieces of paper you don't like.

- How has the tapestry changed? Does it hold together well?
- How do the colors you don't like make the tapestry stronger?
- What parts of me are hardest to like?
- What memories do I try not to think about?
- How am I stronger because of tough times I went through?
- When I feel sad, who can I talk to?
- What happens when I pretend things are OK when they are not OK?

Adolescents and Adults

- What parts of me do I judge to be unacceptable?
- How would I be different if I had not gone through my tough times?
- The story suggests that to be whole, I must integrate all parts of me. How does that make me feel?
- "You can't run away from or get rid of things that are part of you. They are important." Give an example of something you don't like about yourself and how you could turn it into a strength.

CHAPTER 4: CODEPENDENCY

Children

Draw a picture of Samantha the Sheep and her friends Barn Cat, Watch Dog, Milk Cow, and Pig. Draw and cut out a scarf, hat, and sweater to put on Samantha. Discuss how she felt when her friends forgot about her needs.

Draw a family barnyard. Label each animal with the name of someone in your family. Talk about why you picked those names. Then make up a story where the family has to work together to clean up the barnyard. What happens?

- Which animal is most like me?
- Am I more of a giver or more of a taker?
- How do I take good care of myself?
- Why did Samantha give away all her wool?
- What advice do I have for Samantha?
- Which of Samantha's friends do I like the most?

Adolescents and Adults

- How do I know when enough is enough?
- Do I let my friends take advantage of me?

- Are there times I say, "Yes," when I should say, "No"?
- Is it harder for me to give or accept help?
- Where and when did I learn to give others "the wool off my back"?
- In my life, what is the "wool" that I keep giving others?
- Have I ever run out of resources?
- Do I need to stop giving in some area of my life?

CHAPTER 5: PLANNING AHEAD

Children

Draw a picture of Olivia Otter and her friend Jenny doing something exciting but staying safe. Discuss your picture.

- How do I plan ahead?
- How am I like Jenny?
- How am I like Olivia?
- When did I forget to plan ahead and something went wrong? What happened?
- Am I more of an Olivia or more of a Jenny? Why, and give examples.
- What can I do to get more organized?
- Do I take risks and get hurt? What would I need to do to stay safe?

Adolescents and Adults

- How can I have excitement and safety at the same time?
- Am I accident prone?
- What could I do better in order to organize my life or plan ahead?
- How am I like Jenny and Olivia? What advice would Jenny give me?

CHAPTER 6: RECOGNIZING POSITIVES

Children

Write down your "treasures" (strengths) on separate slips of paper. Ask your family members to do the same. Hide them in the house and go on a treasure hunt. When you find them, see if you can figure out who matches each treasure.

- How am I like the people that live in Toss-It-All?
- How am I like the rats?
- Draw a picture of the rats, the town, and the people in it.

- Does my room ever get so messy that I don't know how to clean it up? When I start to clean it, how do I sort the trash from the treasures?
- What are my treasures—things that are special in my life?
- How am I like a treasure?
- Do I feel more like trash or more like treasure? What makes me feel like that?
- Go on a personal treasure hunt inside YOU—make a list of the treasures that make up who you are, such as your strengths and positive attitudes or beliefs.

Adolescents and Adults

- How am I like the people that live in Toss-It-All? How am I like the rats?
- Do I feel more like trash or more like treasure? What makes me feel like that?
- What are some "treasures" that I sometimes overlook?
- Did someone in my life ever make me feel like "trash"?
- Do I focus more on negatives or positives (in others, myself, and life events)?
- Are there specific emotions that blind me from seeing things in a more positive light? (For example, anger, hurt, sadness, or fear)
- Is there someone I have trouble forgiving because I see only the bad?
- Is there a "diamond in the rough" within me that I could polish up?

CHAPTER 7: INTOLERANCE AND PREJUDICE

Children

Draw a picture of the land of Wun.

- Have I ever made fun of someone just for being different?
- Have I been treated with prejudice?
- Have I ever stood up for someone when others were making fun of him or her?
- What are the "in" and "out" groups in my school, family, or neighborhood?
- What do the Wunians need to do to get along better and have peace again?

Adolescents and Adults

- How do I treat those that are different than me?
- When in my life did I first witness or experience prejudice?

- What are the stereotypes people use to justify prejudice?
- How can I be more tolerant or accepting of others?
- Did my parents do anything that instilled prejudice in me?
- Have I done things that made others feel unacceptable?
- How have I experienced rejection for being different?

CHAPTER 8: INFLEXIBILITY

Children

Draw a picture of your "gold" and where you will go to find it.

- How am I like the little girl?
- How am I like the man?
- Do I ever look for things in the wrong place?
- Do I ever get stubborn and refuse to stop what I'm doing, even though it isn't working?

Adolescents and Adults

- In my life, how am I "sifting sand"?
- What is my "gold?" What do I need to do to find it?
- If I "GO for the gold," what is the best thing that could happen? What is the worst thing?
- How will I know I am ready to "GO for the gold"?
- What holds me back from moving in a new direction?
- If I died today, would I have regrets about unfulfilled dreams or things I have not done? What are those things?
- I am powerless to make someone else change. What do I need to do to accept this about someone in my life?
- When do I try to squeeze water out of a rock?

CHAPTER 9: SELF-CONTROL

Children

Draw a picture of your lion on and off his leash.

- How am I like Sam?
- How am I like the lion?
- Parents worry about their children. How do my parents worry about me?

- How did Sam feel when his mother told him to keep the lion on the leash?
- How did Sam's mother feel when he disobeyed?
- How did Sam feel when the lion almost hurt him?
- How did the lion feel on and off the leash? How is his behavior different on and off the leash?
- Pretend to be a lion, on and off his leash. How are you different when you are in control and out of control?

Adolescents and Adults

- What do I need to leash or control in my life?
- Was there a time in my life when I let my "lion" off the "leash"?
- How can I tell when I'm becoming "unleashed"?
- How can I tell when someone else is becoming "unleashed"?
- What are some things that people need to leash or control in their lives?
- What is hardest for me to "leash" inside myself (my own lion)?
- When am I most tempted to unleash my lion?
- How do I feel when I unleash my lion (before, during, and after)?

CHAPTER 10: LETTING GO OF WORRIES

Children

Draw two pictures of Jack—one before and one after he threw away his burdens. How does Jack change?

- How am I like Jack? What advice do I have for Jack?
- What do I worry about the most?
- Talk about a time when you were able to stop worrying and what you did to stop.
- What 3 things do children worry about the most? Do I worry about these things?
- What keeps children from telling adults about their worries?
- What is a worry that I can't or don't talk about?
- Who do I trust to talk with about my worries/problems?
- What are 2 blessings that happened to me this week?
- Make a burden bag backpack out of a paper bag. Color or decorate it. Write down your top 5 burdens. You may use the story categories or create your own. Then put them in the bag. Decide how you will "get rid" of them and carry out that activity.

- What blessings would be in your new backpack? Re-decorate the backpack you made before and fill it with blessings. Take them home and look at them every day!

Adolescents and Adults

- What are 3 burdens (problems/worries) I have carried around for a long time?
- What burden do I most need to get rid of?
- What makes it hard for me to let go of "old baggage"? What steps will I need to take?
- How will I feel when I finally let go of my burdens?
- What burden do I carry around that was not my fault (or was out of my control)?
- Do I pay more attention to blessings or burdens? How can I pay more attention to blessings?

CHAPTER 11: DENIAL AND AVOIDANCE

Children

Draw and color a train track. Paste or draw holes on the track, one for you and one for each other family member. Inside the holes write what each person avoids talking about. It is probably something that is hard to talk about.

- How am I like the ostrich?
- When did I do something dangerous? Did I see the risk?
- How do I know when I am stressed?
- The ostrich put his head in a hole when he was stressed. People do many things to cope with stress to try to feel better (eat, sleep, get in trouble, cry, shout, listen to music, take a walk, etc.). What do I do to try to feel better when I am stressed?
- What are some other things I could do to handle stress?

Adolescents and Adults

- How am I like the ostrich?
- When did someone in my life warn me about something, and I ignored that warning?
- People experience stress in different ways. What stresses me the most?
- When am I most likely to "put my head in the hole"?
- What do I most need to do at this time to better manage my stress?

- Have I ever pretended that the "train" wasn't coming (missed a warning sign that something was wrong, perhaps in my health, a relationship, or at a job)?
- Who in my life would I listen to if they warned me about something I was doing?
- How do I rebel against authority or rules?

CHAPTER 12: PERFORMANCE ANXIETY

Children

Draw a picture of the eagle. Draw another picture of what he fears.

Draw a picture of yourself. Draw another picture of what you fear.

Guided Imagery: Close your eyes and think about Joe the Eagle, finally ready to fly to Tennessee. Pretend you are standing next to Joe the Eagle and giving him some encouragement. As Joe tells you he is nervous, you remind him to relax. Breathe in and out for Joe to show him how to breathe deeply. Remind Joe that even if his heart pounds and his chest gets tight, he can take a deep breath and relax. Show Joe how to take a deep breath and relax. Ask Joe to think about taking off. Remind him to flap his wings slowly, with big, powerful strokes. Show Joe how to move his wings with big, powerful strokes. Tell Joe to take off. Watch Joe take off into the sky. Imagine that you are proud of him and happy for his success. Now, close your eyes. Remind yourself that just like Joe, you can face something you fear. Think about something you have been avoiding or something you fear doing. Remind yourself to breathe deeply and to think encouraging thoughts. Imagine you are successfully doing that very something you fear. At least in your imagination, the fear does not "win." Just like Joe, you have encouraged yourself and now you can fly like an eagle. When you're ready, open your eyes.

- How am I like the eagle?
- How am I like the stork-keeper?
- What are some of my talents or strengths?
- What do I think I am born to be?
- How do I use my talents/strengths?
- What are my biggest fears?
- Who is someone I can talk to about my fears?
- What do I worry about?

Adolescents and Adults

- What are my worst fears? Do they stop me from doing things I need to do?

- What is the worst thing that could happen if my fears came true?
- What am I born to be? What stops me from reaching those dreams or using my talents?
- Was there a time in my life when I let my fears "ground" me? How did I get past my fears?
- Am I more like the eagle or the stork-keeper? How does that make me feel?
- If I allowed myself to soar, what would I do and where would I go?
- We all have special gifts. What are my unique talents?
- Close your eyes. Imagine you are successfully doing something you fear. At least in your imagination, the fear does not "win." How do you feel?
- What do I believe needs to happen or change for me to beat my fear?

CHAPTER 13: PARENTAL MENTAL ILLNESS

Children

- When did I get embarrassed by something my parent did or said?
- Did I ever try to cover up or lie for my parent?
- How is my parent different from other kids' parents?
- Is my parent mentally ill? Why do I think that?
- Do I ever have to take care of my parent?
- Am I afraid that my parent will get too sick to take care of me?
- What are my parent's strengths?
- What do I love most about my parent?

Adolescents and Adults

- Did I or do I have a mentally ill parent? How does that make me feel?
- How do I wish my mentally ill parent would change?
- Have I ever been embarrassed by my parent's inappropriate behavior?
- Did I ever avoid introducing my friends to my parent?
- Did I blame myself for having a mentally ill parent?
- Am I afraid I will become like my parent when I grow older?

CHAPTER 14: FITTING IN SOCIALLY

Children

- How do I have trouble fitting in at school?
- How am I different from other kids my age?
- Everyone has strengths and weaknesses. What are my strengths and in what areas can I work to improve?

- Do I do or say things that make it hard for me to fit in?
- How do I feel when others tease me or make fun of me?
- Am I willing to take the time to "transform" myself?
- Do I believe that people can change? In what areas would I like to change?
- How am I like the main character in the story?

Adolescents and Adults

- How am I like the main character in the story?
- Did I (or do I) have trouble fitting in with those my age?
- Did others tease me because of my odd behavior?
- Do other people ever seem to avoid hanging around with me?
- How old was I when I recognized that I was different than other people my age?
- If I was a transformer, what would my "new and improved" self look like? What would the original "me" look like? Draw a picture of the before and after "you."

CHAPTER 15: BEDTIME ANXIETY

Children

Draw a picture of your favorite part of this story.

- How am I like the girl in this story?
- Am I ever afraid of the dark? If I am, what do I do when I'm afraid?
- When I'm afraid, do I ask anyone for help?
- How and when do I ask for help? How does that make me feel?
- Do I give in to my fears or try to conquer or ignore them?
- How can I stand up to my fears?
- Draw a picture of the girl being brave. Tell 3 things you can do to be brave when you are afraid.
- Make a can of monster spray and try it out.
- Make a string of bells to hang on your bedroom door. Imagine that they can keep out monsters at night.

Adolescents and Adults

- Was I afraid when I was a child? What was I afraid of at that time?
- When I am afraid, do I tell someone or keep it to myself.
- What are my greatest fears at the present time?
- How old do I *feel* when I am frightened?

- Am I still afraid of something I feared as a child? How do I deal with that?
- In coping with my fears, do I "hide," "run for help," "stoically endure," "attack," or "protect/defend myself"?
- As I think about what I fear most, what is the worst thing that could happen if that fear came true?
- What would I do if my fears came true?
- What comforts me when I am afraid?

CHAPTER 16: OBSESSIVE-COMPULSIVE SYMPTOMS

Children

Draw a picture of the frog before and after he gets help. How does he change?

- How am I like the frog?
- Do I have habits that are hard to stop?
- What do I do when I'm worried?
- Do my worries ever keep me from doing things I would like to do?
- When do I feel the most relaxed? What can I do to feel that way more often?
- What can I say to myself to help me worry less?

Hold a smooth "worry stone" and say what you are worried about. Make up some "magic words" and say them. Let the worry travel from your brain through your arm, into your hand, and out of you into the stone. Take a deep breath as you release the worry.

Adolescents and Adults

- Do I have habits/rituals that keep me from enjoying life?
- When am I the most relaxed?
- What would I need to do or change to relax more and enjoy life?
- Do I have secret habits or compulsions that I don't talk about to anyone?
- How do I feel when I can't stop doing something?
- Is there something new I would like to try, but my fears get in the way?
- What in my life is hardest for me to control or change?
- What is my worst "bad habit"?

- Does my worrying help me or hurt me? How does that make me feel?

CHAPTER 17: EATING DISORDERS

Children

- How am I like the girl in this story?
- How do I feel about my own body?
- In what ways do I feel judged by adults?
- Do I have trouble telling my parents or other adults what I really think and feel?
- Do I want to be perfect?
- Does my family have rules? Make a list of your family rules.
- Which rule is my favorite?
- Which rule do I hate the most?
- Is there something I can't talk about with my parents?

Look in a mirror. Imagine your twin criticizing you in some way. What would he or she say? What would you say back? Argue with the twin and stick up for yourself.

Adolescents and Adults

- How am I like the girl in this story?
- How do I feel about my body?
- Do I control how or what I eat to feel better about myself?
- Do I believe that if my weight was different, I would feel better about myself?
- Go to the mall and look around. There are overweight people that are happy and loved. There are thin people that are lonely and unhappy. Do I think I need to be thin to be happy?
- How will I feel if I reach my "perfect" weight and am still unhappy?
- In what ways do I feel controlled by my family?
- Am I more of a pleaser or more of a rebel? Discuss.
- People sometimes believe they would be happier if something changed (if they had more money, had less pain, looked better, lived somewhere else, had a different partner, etc.). Discuss this idea.
- Am I a perfectionist? How does that affect my life?
- Does my family have rules? Which rules do I like? What rule do I most hate?
- Is there something I can't talk about with my parents?

CHAPTER 18: DEPRESSION

Children

Decorate a plastic egg on the outside by covering it in glue and rolling it in sand and gravel. Then on the inside, glue pretty plastic crystals and glitter. Write down your strengths and put them inside the egg. Pretend it is a geode and you discover the beauty inside it. How do you feel?

- How am I like Gerry?
- What advice do I have for Gerry?
- When I think about myself, compared to other kids, do I think I am better, worse, or about the same in . . . my looks, how smart I am, my talents, my physical strength, my athletic ability, making and keeping friends, being popular, and so on?
- What can I do to feel better when I am sad or depressed?

Adolescents and Adults

- How am I like Gerry?
- What advice do I have for Gerry?
- When do I think I'm an ugly rock?
- Have I ever been depressed? How did it affect my mood and attitude?
- What do I need to do to focus on the beauty inside me?

CHAPTER 19: LEARNING DIFFICULTIES

Children

Draw a picture of the puppy.

- How am I like the puppy?
- When do I feel "stupid" even though I'm not?
- How do I feel when I don't know something?
- In what area or areas is it harder for me to learn?
- What does it mean to have a "learning disability"?
- Should the puppy try to swim alone in the storm? Why or why not?
- Is the puppy a bad swimmer? If not, why can't he swim in the storm?

Adolescents and Adults

- What do I feel most inadequate about in terms of my knowledge and abilities?
- In what area(s) do I really struggle to learn?

- Have I ever put myself down or judged myself to be "stupid"?
- What are some of my talents/strengths?
- Do I compare myself to others in a negative way?
- If someone threw me a life jacket (offered me help) in the middle of a hurricane, would I take it? How would it make me feel?
- Have I ever quit something because I thought I might fail?
- Has the fear of failure ever kept me from doing my best?

CHAPTER 20: DIVORCE

Children

Draw a picture of Kit Kat.

- How am I like the kitten in this story?
- How do I feel when my parents argue?
- Do I ever secretly worry that my parents might get a divorce?
- What is the best way for families to work out their problems?
- Has the fighting in my family ever scared me? What scared me the most?
- Do I ever wish my parents would get back together? (If my parents are divorced)

Adolescents and Adults

- Have I ever felt torn by jealousy?
- How did my family handle conflict or anger when I was growing up?
- What are positive ways for people to express angry feelings?
- When parents fight, what effect do I think that has on the children?
- How do I deal with anger or conflict in my current relationships?
- Have I ever been mistreated in a relationship? How did I respond? How do I wish I had responded?
- Have I ever stayed in a relationship, even though it was hurting me?
- Have I ever mistreated someone else?
- How do I feel when a close relationship ends?

CHAPTER 21: PANIC ATTACKS

Children

Draw a picture of the bee and the butterfly.

- How am I a bee and how am I a butterfly?
- What scares me the most and where do I "hide"?

- Did the butterfly made a good decision when she went to hide in the woods?
- What can the butterfly do to feel better the next time she sees a bird or a dog?
- What do I need to do to get over my fears?
- How am I like the bee, and how am I like the butterfly? How am I different from each of them?

Adolescents and Adults

- How am I a bee and how am I a butterfly?
- How/where do I hide from my fears?
- What do I think would happen to the butterfly if she stayed in the cave the rest of her life?
- What advice would I give the butterfly? What do I think of the bee's advice?
- Under what conditions would I use my stinger, knowing I would then die?
- When do I feel fragile and vulnerable?
- In my past, was I ever trapped by my fears? Was I ever "brave" in spite of my fears?
- Was I afraid when I was a child? What was I afraid of at that time?
- When I am afraid, do I tell someone or keep it to myself?
- What are my greatest fears at the present time?
- How old do I *feel* when I am frightened?
- Am I still afraid of something I feared as a child? How do I deal with that?
- In coping with my fears, do I "hide," "run for help," "stoically endure," "attack," or "protect/defend myself"?
- As I think about what I fear most, what is the worst thing that could happen if that fear came true? What would I do if my fears came true?
- What comforts me when I am afraid?

CHAPTER 22: ATTENTION DEFICIT SYMPTOMS

Children

Draw a picture of the girl and her magic glasses.

- How am I like the girl in the story?
- What advice do I have for the girl in the story?
- When did I lie to my parents because I was afraid of getting in trouble?

- What can a child do to feel better when he/she is upset?
- Have I ever kept a secret when I should have told someone?

Adolescents and Adults

- How and when do I wear "magic glasses"?
- What things are hard for me to accept about myself?
- What can I do to "take off my glasses" and accept myself?
- What do I "hide" or keep secret about myself?

Appendix B

Squiggles Stories

It helps to get permission from a parent or guardian as well as the child prior to beginning this work in order to photograph the finished drawings. That way the drawings may be preserved and condensed into a PowerPoint file.

- To begin squiggles, therapist closes eyes and makes a simple squiggle on the dry erase board (or on a piece of paper).
- Therapist hands the paper to the child, asking him or her to *complete* the squiggle (turn it into a drawing). The child is given dry erase markers of many colors. Therapist watches closely, noting colors used, changes made (sometimes a defensive strategy), and comments by the child.
- When finished, the child is asked to tell a TAT-like story about the drawing—a story not yet heard, with a beginning, middle, and end. I ask questions as needed about what the characters are thinking, feeling, and doing.
- While the children tells the story, the therapist listens carefully for themes, parallels to the child's life, wishes or fantasies, coping skills, problem-solving strategies, and intensity of feelings.
- Once the child finishes his or her story, the therapist asks the child for permission to photograph the finished drawing.
- The child is asked to do a squiggle for the therapist.
- Therapist completes the squiggle and tells a story. The story may parallel the child's, add new problem-solving elements, include interpretive information, challenge the child's conclusions, etc.

The therapist and child *trading* squiggles and stories back and forth will springboard the child into a discussion of real life events. Over time, it allows the child to make changes in views and feelings about self, others, and the world.

Like mutual storytelling, this process elicits significant client concerns, client hopes and dreams, client problem-solving processes, and client irrational beliefs. One of my first child clients in 1978, who was using squiggles and storytelling to deal with his anger, provided the character for *The Dragon's Fire*. Another client used her squiggles story to begin her trauma narrative and proceeded to work on her abuse and neglect issues. The technique, using a dry erase board, is an excellent one for less verbal or cognitively challenged children and teens.

References

Alexander, James. *Functional family therapy*. University of Utah, Department of Psychology.

Cohen, J. A., Mannarino, A. P., & Deblinger, E. 2003. *Child and parent trauma-focused cognitive behavioral therapy manual.*

Drewes, A., ed. 2009. *Blending play therapy with cognitive behavioral therapy: Evidence-based and other effective treatments and techniques*. New York: Wiley.

Elliott, Jane. http://en.wikipedia.org/wiki/Jane_Elliott (accessed 2/6/10).

Gardner, R. 1971. *Therapeutic communication with children: The mutual storytelling technique*. New York: Science House.

Gil, E. 2006. *Helping abused and traumatized children: Integrating directive and nondirective approaches*. New York: The Guilford Press.

———. 1994. *Play in family therapy*. New York: The Guilford Press.

Gurney, Bernard, & Gurney, Louise. 1964. *Filial therapy*.

Herschell, A., Calzada, E., Eyberg, S. M., & McNeil, C. B. 2002. "Parent-child interaction therapy: New directions in research." *Cognitive and Behavioral Practice* 9: 9–16.

Kendall, P. & Hedtke, K. 2006 *Coping cat workbook, 2nd edition (ages 7–13)*. Workbook Publishing, Inc.

O'Hanlon, B. 1993. "Solution-oriented hypnosis for inner healing." Workshop. Nashville, IN: Solutions, Inc.

Pavuluri, M. RAINBOW Treatment Program, University of Illinois at Chicago.

Schaefer, C. E., and K. O'Connor. 1983. *Handbook of play therapy*. New York: Wiley.

Seligman, M., and M. Csikszentmihalyi. 2000. Positive psychology: An introduction. *American Psychologist* 55(1):5–14.

Zeig, J. 2008. "The Utilization of Ericksonian Methods in Couples and Family Therapy." Workshop. Louisville, Kentucky.

Index

About the Author

Pat Pernicano, PsyD, is director of clinical services at Providence Self Sufficiency Ministries, where she provides programmatic direction and clinical supervision for the Family Preservation Program and Providence House for Children Group Homes. Dr. Pernicano is also a clinical faculty member at Spalding University and teaches part-time in the PsyD program.

www.ingramcontent.com/pod-product-compliance
Ingram Content Group UK Ltd.
Pitfield, Milton Keynes, MK11 3LW, UK
UKHW012042150926
475560UK00001B/147

9 780765 70781